SpringerBriefs in Computer Science

SpringerBriefs present concise summaries of cutting-edge research and practical applications across a wide spectrum of fields. Featuring compact volumes of 50 to 125 pages, the series covers a range of content from professional to academic.

Typical topics might include:

- A timely report of state-of-the art analytical techniques
- A bridge between new research results, as published in journal articles, and a contextual literature review
- A snapshot of a hot or emerging topic
- An in-depth case study or clinical example
- A presentation of core concepts that students must understand in order to make independent contributions

Briefs allow authors to present their ideas and readers to absorb them with minimal time investment. Briefs will be published as part of Springer's eBook collection, with millions of users worldwide. In addition, Briefs will be available for individual print and electronic purchase. Briefs are characterized by fast, global electronic dissemination, standard publishing contracts, easy-to-use manuscript preparation and formatting guidelines, and expedited production schedules. We aim for publication 8–12 weeks after acceptance. Both solicited and unsolicited manuscripts are considered for publication in this series.

**Indexing: This series is indexed in Scopus, Ei-Compendex, and zbMATH **

Jiadi Yu • Hao Kong • Linghe Kong

WiFi signal-based user authentication

 Springer

Jiadi Yu
Department of CS and Engineering
Shanghai Jiao Tong University
Shanghai, China

Hao Kong
School of Computer Engineering
and Science
Shanghai University
Shanghai, China

Linghe Kong
Department of CS and Engineering
Shanghai Jiao Tong University
Shanghai, China

ISSN 2191-5768   ISSN 2191-5776   (electronic)
SpringerBriefs in Computer Science
ISBN 978-981-99-5913-6   ISBN 978-981-99-5914-3   (eBook)
https://doi.org/10.1007/978-981-99-5914-3

This Springer imprint is published by the registered company Springer Nature Singapore Pte Ltd.
The registered company address is: 152 Beach Road, #21-01/04 Gateway East, Singapore 189721,
Singapore

Paper in this product is recyclable.

Preface

With the continuous progress of Internet of Things (IoT) technology and the wide application of artificial intelligence, Artificial Intelligence of Things (AIoT) is gradually popularized in daily life. Applications of AIoT are characterized by data informatization and service customization. Unauthorized access to these information and services could cause potential information security risks. Therefore, for the high security requirements of data, applications, and services, user authentication has become an indispensable security guarantee.

Existing biometrics-based identification methods, such as face recognition, fingerprint recognition, and vocalprint recognition, are facing the threat of biometric theft and replay attacks. Previous works have built user authentication methods based on WiFi signals. These works leverage WiFi signals to sense human behavioral features for user authentication, providing a non-intrusive solution that can naturally resist theft and replay attacks. However, these works lack sufficient exploration and research on the diversity of user behaviors and the complexity of scenarios in real use. Facing the challenges in existing approaches, this book presents a new approach of WiFi signal-based user authentication toward diversified behaviors and complex scenarios.

This book begins by introducing user authentication approaches and the development of WiFi signal sensing technology in Chap. 1. We also present the motivation behind the book and summarize our contributions. After that, in Chap. 2, we propose a finger gesture-based user authentication using WiFi signals, which integrates human-computer interaction and user authentication. The proposed *FingerPass* leverages WiFi signals to sense finger gestures. It divides the authentication process into two states, i.e., identification stage and interaction stage, to ensure high accuracy and real-time response in the authentication process. It is evaluated in indoor environments and demonstrated effectiveness in finger gesture-based user authentication. In Chap. 3, we discuss gesture-independent authentication problem and propose a *FreeAuth* to realize user authentication toward undefined gestures. The proposed *FreeAuth* utilizes a generative adversarial network to suppress specific behavioral features and extract invariant individual uniqueness. We evaluate the system in real indoor environments and prove its capability in gesture-independent user authentication. In Chap. 4, we exploit the feasibility of multi-user authentication using WiFi signals. We propose a *MultiAuth* system, which leverages WiFi signals to sense multiple users simultaneously for user authentication. *MultiAuth* performs multipath profiling to separate the signals of multiple users and construct a synthetic signal component for each user. Employing a deep neural network to extract behavioral features, *MultiAuth* can realize WiFi signal-based multi-user authentication. We evaluate the system in real multi-user scenarios and it achieves effective performance. In Chap. 5, we provide an overview of the state-of-the-art research. Finally, a summary of the book and future research directions are presented in Chap. 6.

Shanghai, People's Republic of China   Jiadi Yu
July 2023   Hao Kong
                                                                                             Linghe Kong

Contents

Chapter 1
Overview

Abstract The development of smart homes has advanced the concept of user authentication to not only protecting user privacy but also facilitating personalized services to users. Along this direction, we propose to integrate user authentication with human-computer interactions between users and smart household appliances through widely-deployed WiFi infrastructures, which is non-intrusive and device-free. This chapter proposes a *FingerPass* system, which leverages channel state information (CSI) of WiFi signals to continuously authenticate users through finger gestures. We first investigate CSI of WiFi signals in depth and find CSI phase can be used to capture and distinguish the unique behavioral characteristics from different users. *FingerPass* separates the user authentication process into two stages, login and interaction, to achieve high authentication accuracy and low response latency simultaneously. In the login stage, we develop a deep learning-based approach to extract behavioral characteristics of finger gestures for highly accurate user identification. For the interaction stage, to provide continuous authentication in real time for satisfactory user experience, we design a verification mechanism with lightweight classifiers to continuously authenticate the user's identity. With extensive experiments, this chapter demonstrate that *FingerPass* achieves accurate user authentication with real-time response during interactions.

Keywords User authentication · Finger gesture · WiFi signals · Smart home

1.1 Brief Introduction of User Authentication

User authentication generally refers to the technology of identifying and verifying user identity by certain means. In recent years, as more and more IoT devices have appeared and people use these devices to store personal sensitive and private data, the protection of data security and personal privacy has become particularly important, which has prompted the widespread demand for user authentication.

In extensive application scenarios, traditional user authentication methods still play an important role. Traditional identification methods include password, Personal Identification Number (PIN), entity ID card, token authentication, etc. They

© The Author(s), under exclusive license to Springer Nature Singapore Pte Ltd. 2023   1
J. Yu et al., *WiFi signal-based user authentication*, SpringerBriefs in Computer
Science, https://doi.org/10.1007/978-981-99-5914-3_1

have achieved huge access in ensuring data security of account control. Nowadays, biometrics-based user authentication has attached tons of attention. Biometrics-based method can authenticate users based on their physiological characteristics by perceiving and extracting biological features. For example, unique fingerprint patterns, texture features of the iris, facial features, voice features, etc., have become popular biometrics for user authentication. This has yielded a surge of commercial devices in fingerprint recognition, iris recognition, face recognition, and voiceprint recognition. Biometric-based user authentication is widely used in IoT environments owing to the efficiency and availability. They naturally avoid the potential threat that traditional methods are easy to discard.

In recent years, signal-based user authentication appears. Signal-based methods leverage ubiquitous signals to sense human behavioral features for user authentication. These signals include mechanical wave signals (such as acoustic signals) and radio frequency signals (such as RIFD, millimeter wave, WiFi, etc.). Existing mobile devices are generally equipped with voice modules, which promotes the development of acoustic signal-based user authentication. For example, acoustic signals can sense the movement of user's mouth to authentication users during lip-reading. In addition, acoustic signals can also sense the inherent physiological characteristics of the vocal tract when speaking to achieve content-independent authentication. Radio frequency signals, such as RFID, millimeter wave (mmWave) signals, and WiFi signals, are also suitable in user authentication. For example, we can use the characteristics of RFID to passively sense unique gait features for user authentication. We can use mmWave signals to sense facial features, vocal channel features, or heartbeat features for user authentication. In addition, the widespread presence of WiFi signals also produces WiFi signal-based user authentication. Since WiFi signals are almost ubiquitous in IoT environments, they have become one the most low-cost and natural manner to sense behavioral features for user authentication. Leveraging WiFi signals to sense a user's walking activity can extract unique behavioral features such as stride length and frequency. In addition to human gait, daily activities can also be used for user authentication, such as hand gestures, body gestures, typing, etc.

1.2 Development of WiFi Signal Sensing

WiFi is one of the technologies built for indoor wireless networks. Based on IEEE 802.11, combined with Multiple Input Multiple Output (MIMO), Orthogonal Frequency Division Multiplexing (OFDM) and other technologies, WiFi provides high transmission rate, wide coverage, and low cost wireless capabilities. This makes all kinds of WiFi devices continue to appear in IoT environments, becoming the main force to support wireless networks. In addition, more and more traditional devices are also equipped with WiFi modules to connect various traditional devices into IoT ecosystem. The widespread popularity of WiFi devices has led to another key function in addition to wireless network communication, i.e., WiFi signal sensing.

It refers to the acquisition of target (such as environment, human body, equipment) information through the propagation of WiFi signal in space. Combined with machine learning methods, WiFi signal sensing has produced a broad applications, such as indoor positioning, behavior recognition, user authentication, etc.

Received Signal Strength (RSS) of WiFi signals is a key sensing technology. The basic principle is that the presence and activity of the target will cause a change of signal strength during the propagation of WiFi signals. Hence, the target can be sensed through measuring the change of RSS data. However, RSS is only a coarse-grained description of signal strength, which is susceptible to multipath effects and limits its sensing ability. In recent years, researchers propose open source tools for commercial WiFi network card that can read Channel State Information (CSI) during wireless communication. CSI describes the characteristics of communication link in the wireless communication process, including power attenuation, signal scattering in each channel, etc. Compared with RSS, CSI can estimate specific channel information, characterize the frequency selective fading characteristics of WiFi channels, and distinguish the multipath components. Hence, it has more powerful sensing capability. Based on the widespread existence of WiFi devices, a series of sensing applications based on WiFi signals are emerged. For example, we can use WiFi signal to achieve device-based indoor positioning, device-free human behavior recognition, gesture recognition, indoor positioning, breath monitoring, user authentication, key recognition, etc. This has proved the research boom of WiFi signal sensing technologies and applications.

1.3 Overview of the Book

In this book, we elaborate on the studies on WiFi signal-based user authentication based on realistic data collected in real indoor environments. The reminder of this book is organized as follows:

In Chap. 2, we propose to integrate user authentication with human-computer interactions between users and smart household appliances through widely-deployed WiFi infrastructures, which is nonintrusive and device-free. We propose a *FingerPass* system, which leverages CSI of surrounding WiFi signals to continuously authenticate users through finger gestures in smart homes. We investigate CSI of WiFi signals in depth and find CSI phase can be used to capture and distinguish the unique behavioral characteristics from different users. *FingerPass* separates the user authentication process into two stages, login and interaction, to achieve high authentication accuracy and low response latency simultaneously. In the login stage, we develop a deep learning-based approach to extract behavioral characteristics of finger gestures for highly accurate user identification. For the interaction stage, to provide continuous authentication in real time for satisfactory user experience, we design a verification mechanism with lightweight classifiers to continuously authenticate the user's identity during each interaction of finger gestures. Extensive experiments involving 7 participants in real environments show that *FingerPass* can achieve effective user authentication with a low response time during the interaction.

In Chap. 3, we aim to enable WiFi-based user authentication with undefined body gestures rather than only predefined body gestures, i.e., realizing a gesture-independent user authentication. We first explore physiological characteristics underlying body gestures, and find that statistical distributions under WiFi signals induced by body gestures can exhibit invariant individual uniqueness unrelated to specific body gestures. Inspired by this observation, we propose a user authentication system, *FreeAuth*, which utilizes WiFi signals to identify individuals in a gesture-independent manner. Specifically, we design an adversarial learning-based model, which suppresses specific gesture characteristics, and extracts invariant individual uniqueness unrelated to specific body gestures, to authenticate users in a gesture-independent manner. Extensive experiments in indoor environments involving 30 participants show that the proposed system is feasible and effective in gesture-independent user authentication.

In Chap. 4, we present a multi-user authentication system, *MultiAuth*, which can authenticate multiple users with a single commodity WiFi device. The key idea is to profile multipath components of WiFi signals induced by multiple users, and construct individual CSI from the multipath components to solely characterize each user for user authentication. Specifically, we propose a MUltipath Time-of-Arrival measurement algorithm (MUTA) to profile multipath components of WiFi signals in high resolution. Then, after aggregating and separating the multipath components related to users, *MultiAuth* constructs individual CSI based on the multipath components to solely characterize each user. To identify users, *MultiAuth* further extracts user behavior profiles based on the individual CSI of each user through time-frequency analysis, and leverages a dual-task neural network for robust user authentication. Extensive experiments involving 30 users demonstrate that *MultiAuth* is accurate and reliable for multi-user authentication with up to 3 users are simultaneously presented.

In Chap. 5, we give a brief review of state-of-art works related to the approaches presented in this book. This chapter starts with introducing the representative researches of user authentication. Then researches focusing on WiFi signal sensing are mentioned. After that, we gives introduction to WiFi signal-based user authentication research in recent decades. Finally, we present challenges of existing research and the difference between them and this book.

In Chap. 6, we show that works presented in this book identifies new problems and solutions of WiFi signal-based user authentication, which helps us to advance our understanding WiFi sensing and its applications related to user authentication. We present the future direction of our research at the end of the book.

Chapter 2
Finger Gesture-Based Continuous User Authentication Using WiFi

Abstract The development of smart homes has advanced the concept of user authentication to not only protecting user privacy but also facilitating personalized services to users. Along this direction, we propose to integrate user authentication with human-computer interactions between users and smart household appliances through widely-deployed WiFi infrastructures, which is non-intrusive and device-free. This chapter proposes a *FingerPass* system, which leverages channel state information (CSI) of WiFi signals to continuously authenticate users through finger gestures. We first investigate CSI of WiFi signals in depth and find CSI phase can be used to capture and distinguish the unique behavioral characteristics from different users. *FingerPass* separates the user authentication process into two stages, login and interaction, to achieve high authentication accuracy and low response latency simultaneously. In the login stage, we develop a deep learning-based approach to extract behavioral characteristics of finger gestures for highly accurate user identification. For the interaction stage, to provide continuous authentication in real time for satisfactory user experience, we design a verification mechanism with lightweight classifiers to continuously authenticate the user's identity. With extensive experiments, this chapter demonstrates that *FingerPass* achieves accurate user authentication with real-time response during interactions.

Keywords User authentication · Finger gesture · WiFi signals · Smart home

2.1 Introduction

With the development of IoT, smart household appliances are increasingly pervasive and common in home environments, making smart homes a practical realization. According to a report [8], the global smart Home automation market was valued at USD 75.9 Bn in 2021 and is anticipated to grow at a CAGR of 14.4% and is expected to reach USD 254.7 Bn by 2030. Smart household appliances store various sensitive information such as personal interests, hygiene habits, health status, which could facilitate a variety of customized services. However, such potentially leaked information could cause unauthorized access to personal data and derivation of personal lifestyles. Thus, it is essential to provide secure user access to smart appliances in home environments.

Existing user authentication approaches, such as fingerprint [3], voiceprint [20], and face recognition [12], are widely deployed in today's typical and IoT scenarios. Although these biometrics-based approaches are successful, they may suffer from replay attacks. In addition, they only provide one-off user authentication, which are unsuitable for continuous privacy protection. To provide continuous protection for privacy and security in smart homes, some works [10, 18] exploit human behavioral features underlying human computer interaction and implement behavior-based user authentication. But these methods usually need wearable sensors or specialized infrastructure, introducing intrusive user experience and high cost. Recently, WiFi infrastructures are widely deployed and WiFi signals are almost everywhere in indoor environments. Hence, researchers [13, 19] utilize WiFi signals to sense human activities for user authentication. However, existing approaches rely on coarse-grained human movements (e.g., gaits, daily activities).

In smart homes, fine-grained finger gestures are a more natural and common way for human-computer interactions. Users usually perform various finger gestures to interact with machines. Toward this end, this chapter presents a finger gesture-based continuous user authentication system using WiFi signals, which achieves continuous privacy protection in smart homes. To implement the system, we face several challenges in practice. First, the system needs to mitigate interference induced by unconscious finger motions in CSI of WiFi signals to extract robust features. Second, we should extract unique behavioral features and accurately authenticate users for secure access control. Finally, we should provide real-time response in the interaction-based user authentication for satisfactory user experience.

In this chapter, we first explore using WiFi signals to sense finger gestures for user authentication. We extract Channel State Information (CSI) of WiFi signals and observe that CSI phase of WiFi signals captures behavioral characteristics of users. Based on the observation, we propose a finger gesture-based continuous user authentication system, *FingerPass*, which leverages WiFi signals to continuously authenticate users with finger gestures. First, *FingerPass* pre-processes the received CSI of WiFi signals and segments the signals into episodes through amplitude differential, and then recognizes different finger gestures through Support Vector Machine (SVM). To ensure accuracy and user experience, the whole authentication process of *FingerPass* is divided into two stages, i.e., the login and interaction stages. The login stage identifies a user from multiple registered users, which utilizes Long Short-Term Memory-based Deep Neural Network (LSTM-based DNN) extract unique behavioral characteristics. After a successful login, the user further interacts with the system in the interaction stage. To provide continuous protection in real time, *FingerPass* verifies the user's identity during each interaction of finger gestures by a verification mechanism based on lightweight Support Vector Domain Description (SVDD). Experiments demonstrate that *FingerPass* is effective in continuous user authentication.

The rest of the chapter is organized as follows. Sect. 2.2 gives a preliminary analysis. Then, we present the detailed system design of *FingerPass* in Sect. 2.3. Sect. 2.4 provides the evaluation of the system. The chapter ends with a conclusion in Sect. 2.5.

2.2 Preliminary

In this section, we first describe attack scenarios in smart homes, and then explore the feasibility of WiFi signal-based continuous user authentication.

2.2.1 Attack Scenarios in Smart Homes

As the popularity of smart homes, smart household appliances would not only store individual privacy, but also provide personalized services for specific family members. Traditional user authentication for smart household appliances is usually a one-off process, i.e., authenticate user's identity only once during login. However, users usually do not log out such smart household appliances when they are temporarily suspended. This may result in two representative attack scenarios in smart homes. The first scenario is that the individual information may be leaked to adversaries. For example, a malicious guest in the home may eavesdrop privacies of family members from smart household appliances. The second scenario is that the personalized services provided for specific users may be mistakenly provided to other unsuitable users. For example, children may interact with smart household appliances out of curiosity during the absence of adults, which makes it possible for children to use unsuitable services (e.g., adult movie, online shopping, etc.). The traditional user authentication cannot provide a continuous guarantee for privacy protection to prevent the two attack scenarios. Therefore, it is necessary to secure each interaction between users and smart household appliances, i.e., enable a continuous user authentication during the use of smart household appliances.

2.2.2 Feasibility of Finger Gesture-Based Authentication

The Channel State Information (CSI) of WiFi signals [4] describes the channel properties of a WiFi signal's propagating path, which can be utilized to recognize different finger gestures by CSI amplitude [7, 16]. Hence, we first investigate the feasibility of utilizing CSI amplitude of WiFi signals for finger gesture-based user authentication.

To validate whether CSI amplitude can be used to distinguish different users, we conduct an experiment involving two volunteers in a lab. Each volunteer is required

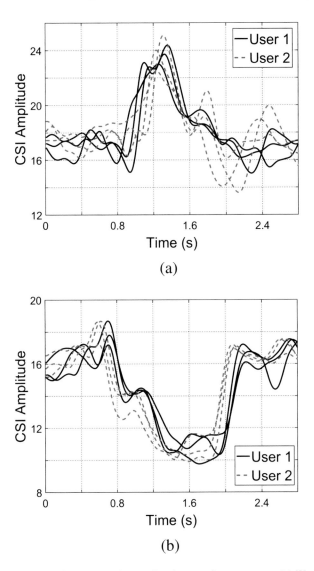

Fig. 2.1 CSI Amplitude of two users when performing two finger gestures. (**a**) Waving right. (**b**) Circling left

to perform two different finger gestures (i.e., waving right and circling left) three times. There is a wireless Access Point (TP-LINK-WDR5620) and a laptop (HP Pavilion 14) equipped with Intel WiFi Link 5300 NIC. The distance between the AP and the laptop is 1 m. The finger gestures are required to be conducted in the middle of the two devices. Figure 2.1 shows CSI amplitude at 20th subcarrier when two volunteers perform two different finger gestures three times respectively. We can see that there are significant differences on CSI amplitudes for the two finger gestures, which is consistent with existing works [7, 16]. However, the differences between different users are not distinct enough to separate the curves, which indicates that the CSI amplitude cannot be used to distinguish different users. This is because subtle differences between users are overridden by the differences between different finger gestures. Specifically, a finger gesture blocks the propagating path of WiFi signals between a transmitter and a receiver, which induces significant energy attenuation of received WiFi signals. Thus, the CSI amplitude would change significantly due to the energy attenuation. However, since the finger blockage depicts the coarse-grained characteristics of finger gestures, it would override the fine-grained behavioral uniquenesses of different users, i.e., the subtle differences between users cannot be exhibited in CSI amplitude of WiFi signals.

In order to distinguish different users through CSI of WiFi signals, we consider another measure, i.e., CSI phase of WiFi signals, which can express the movement of an object in the propagating path of WiFi signals [17]. However, the absolute CSI phase has an unpredictable offset due to hardware imperfection [21]. Hence, we employ relative phase to eliminate the offset and further reveal fine-grained behavioral characteristics. The relative phase at the kth subcarrier can be represented as:

$$\angle \hat{H}_k = -\frac{2\pi}{\lambda} \Delta d, \tag{2.1}$$

where Δd is the length difference of two transmitting paths, and λ is the signal wavelength. The relative phase can reveal more fine-grained behavioral characteristics due to the cm-scale λ [13].

To explore the feasibility of user authentication through CSI phase of WiFi signals, we analyze the data collected from the previous experiment. Figure 2.2 shows the relative phase of WiFi signals when the two volunteers perform the two finger gestures respectively. Different from CSI amplitude, there are differences between different users when performing the same finger gesture, which can be used to distinguish different users. The result indicates that utilizing CSI phase of WiFi signals is feasible to authenticate user's identity. This is because the differences between different users mainly depend on behavioral characteristics, such as moving distance, speed, and orientation of a user's fingers and palm. The moving fingers and palm reflect WiFi signals, which would change the length of a propagating path of the WiFi signals. Such a length change of propagating path can be exhibited as CSI phase shift of WiFi signals [1]. This indicates that the CSI phase of received WiFi signals describes the behavioral characteristics of finger gestures, which can be further used to authenticate users.

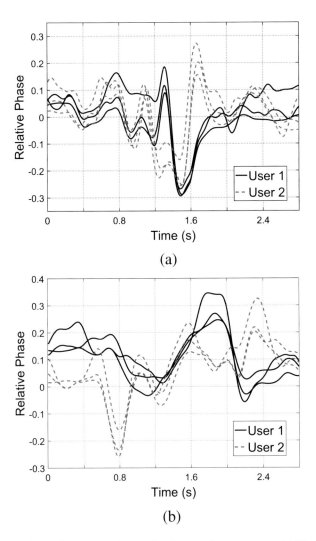

Fig. 2.2 Relative phase of two users when performing two finger gestures. (**a**) Waving right. (**b**) Circling left

2.2.3   Finger Gesture-Based Continuous User Authentication in Real Time

We aim to integrate user authentication into finger gesture-based interactions with smart household appliances, which enables continuous user authentication. Designing the user authentication system with a satisfactory user experience is crucial. Users usually expect real-time responses when interacting with smart household appliances, rather than experiencing long delays. Therefore, continuous user authentication should meet the real-time response requirement to ensure a satisfactory user experience. In order to achieve real-time response, we start by considering the workflow of a typical human-computer interaction system that includes one-off user authentication. The initial step in this system is the identification process for user login, which involves solving a multi-class problem. Once the login is successful, all subsequent services are provided based on the identity of the logged-in user. To extend this typical system to continuous user authentication, we introduce a verification process during each interaction. This process checks whether the current user is the logged-in user or not, essentially making the user authentication during interactions a binary classification task.

To achieve continuous authentication while meeting real-time requirements, we divide the authentication process into two stages: the login stage and the interaction stage, which correspond to user identification and verification, respectively. During the login stage, the user's identity is identified through a specific finger gesture, which is a one-time process. Since there are minimal interaction requests from users at this stage, a relatively longer response time can be tolerated to achieve high accuracy identification without significant degradation of the user experience. In the interaction stage, the system verifies the identity of the current user based on each finger gesture interaction. To ensure a satisfactory user experience during these interactions, the system needs to respond in real time to the finger gestures, providing instantaneous feedback.

Implementing finger gesture-based continuous user authentication through WiFi signals presents practical challenges. The first challenge involves the CSI phase of WiFi signals affected by finger gestures. The phase contains both behavioral characteristics and unconscious motions induced by finger movement that cannot accurately represent user characteristics. Therefore, it is crucial to extract the unique features related to behavioral characteristics to ensure robust user identification during the login stage. The second challenge pertains to user verification during interactions while maintaining a satisfactory user experience. To achieve real-time response, a lightweight method can be employed. However, using such a lightweight method for user verification may impact the overall authentication performance due to inherent limitations of the method. Consequently, it is necessary to explore a verification mechanism that balances both verification accuracy and real-time response during interactions.

2.3 System Design

In this section, we present the design of *FingerPass*, which leverages CSI of WiFi signals to continuously authenticate users based on finger gestures with high accuracy and real-time response.

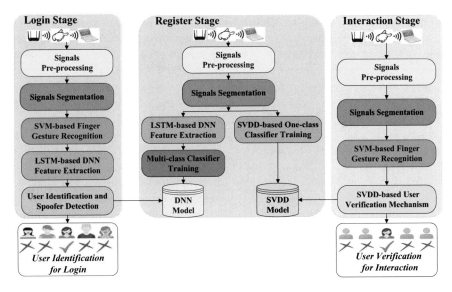

Fig. 2.3 Architecture of *FingerPass*

2.3.1 System Overview

Figure 2.3 shows the architecture of the system, which includes a register stage, a login stage, and an interaction stage. The register stage is an off-line training process, and the login and interaction stages are on-line authentication processes.

During the register stage, the system collects multiple finger gestures from family members to train the model for user identification and verification. First, the received WiFi signals are processed by *FingerPass* to mitigate multipath effects. This is achieved through techniques such as Inverse Fast Fourier Transform (IFFT) and Butterworth filtering. Specifically, specific subcarriers that are sensitive to movements are selected. Next, the pre-processed signals are segmented into episodes of finger gestures based on the amplitude differential observed in the received WiFi signals. *FingerPass* utilizes a Long Short-Term Memory-based Deep Neural Network (LSTM-based DNN) to construct a DNN model. This model is trained for user identification during the login stage, leveraging the extracted features from the finger gesture episodes. Finally, Support Vector Domain Description (SVDD) is employed to construct a lightweight SVDD model. This model is specifically designed for user verification during interactions. The SVDD model aims to balance the need for real-time response with verification accuracy, ensuring an efficient and reliable authentication process.

During the login stage, the signals are processed and segmented following the same procedure as in the register stage. Next, *FingerPass* employs Support Vector Machine (SVM) based on CSI amplitude to recognize the login finger gestures. Afterwards, *FingerPass* extracts unique behavioral characteristics of the user from the CSI phase using LSTM-based DNN feature extraction. These features capture the individual's specific behavioral patterns, which are then used for user identification and spoofer detection. The trained DNN model plays a crucial role in accurately identifying the user and distinguishing between legitimate users and potential spoofers.

In the interaction stage, each finger gesture is considered as an interaction request. *FingerPass* processes and segments the signals received during the interaction. Finger gestures are then recognized using the established techniques. To provide continuous user authentication during finger gesture-based interactions, a verification mechanism is employed. This mechanism utilizes the trained SVDD models and is specifically designed for lightweight and efficient verification. It ensures that the user authentication process remains secure and reliable throughout the interactions.

2.3.2   Signal Pre-processing

In this section, we first describe techniques to mitigate multipath effects, and then present selecting sensitive subcarriers.

2.3.2.1   Multipath Mitigation

Multipath effects may interfere with the received WiFi signals, which could potentially reduce the robustness of finger gesture-based user authentication. To address this issue, mitigating the multipath effect from received WiFi signals becomes necessary. One approach is to remove signal components with a large time delay, which typically originate from distant dynamic movements. This approach has been explored in previous studies, such as [16], where it was found that indoor environments usually have a maximum delay of less than 500 ns [6]. To mitigate the multipath effect, we employ the power delay profile obtained through the n-point Inverse Fast Fourier Transform (IFFT) on the CSI of WiFi signals at each subcarrier in the frequency domain. By removing signal components with a large delay in the power delay profile, we can effectively mitigate multipath effects caused by distant dynamic movements. It is worth noting that the IFFT operation reduces the time resolution of the received WiFi signals. However, the mitigation of multipath effects through IFFT contributes significantly to resisting interference from ambient moving objects and ultimately improves the robustness of user authentication.

2.3.2.2   Subcarriers Selection

WiFi infrastructures typically provide multiple subcarriers for communication, but not all of them are equally sensitive in sensing. Some subcarriers may be insensitive to specific environmental changes, which reduces the contribution to capturing the unique features of human movement [13]. To address this, *FingerPass* selects sensitive subcarriers from the total of m subcarriers present in the CSI of WiFi signals. This selection process helps reduce the coverage of insensitive subcarriers and focuses on those that are more effective in capturing the unique characteristics of finger gestures. Specifically, *FingerPass* selects k subcarriers whose variance values exceed the mean variance values as sensitive subcarriers. The variance values serve as indicators of sensitivity. For each sensitive subcarrier, the proportion of its variance value, represented as w_i, is used as a weight to combine the information from each subcarrier. This combination process yields a combined sensitive subcarrier. Given $W = \sum_{i=1}^{k} w_i$ which represents the sum of sensitive subcarriers' variance values, the combined carrier H is calculated as $H = \sum_{i=1}^{k} \frac{w_i}{W} H_i$, where H_i denotes CSI of ith subcarrier. By leveraging the combined subcarrier with high sensitivity to finger gestures, *FingerPass* enhances the feature extraction process, enabling the capture of unique behavioral characteristics specific to users.

2.3.3 Finger Gesture Detection and Recognition

In this section, we describe signal segmentation and gesture recognition.

2.3.3.1 Signals Segmentation

Different finger gestures would induce different values on CSI amplitude. In the top part of Fig. 2.4, we can observe the CSI amplitude of WiFi signals induced by two different finger gestures. However, when comparing the first finger gesture to the second one, the amplitude value of the first finger gesture is less pronounced and can be similar to the white noise present in the CSI amplitude. This similarity between the first finger gesture and white noise can introduce challenges in detecting certain finger gestures accurately. Additionally, it can lead to the mistaken detection of white noise as a finger gesture. Despite these challenges, it is worth noting that the CSI amplitude induced by different finger gestures still exhibits significant changes. This observation allows us to consider utilizing the amplitude change as a means of segmenting the signals effectively. By leveraging the amplitude change as a segmentation criterion, we can enhance the accuracy of detecting finger gestures and differentiate them from background noise.

To depict the change of CSI amplitude, we define *amplitude differential*, i.e.,

$$D(n) = \sum_{t=nL}^{(n+1)L-1} |(C_{t+1} - C_t)|, \quad n \in [0, N-1], \tag{2.2}$$

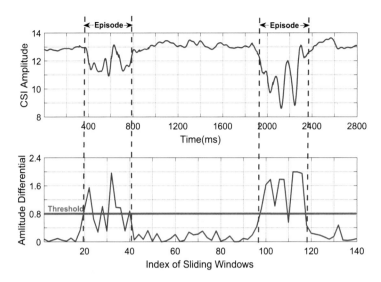

Fig. 2.4 Illustration of signals segmentation leveraging amplitude differential

where $D(n)$ denotes the amplitude differential of nth sliding window, L is the length of a sliding window, C_t is a CSI amplitude value at time t, and N is the number of sliding windows. The bottom part of Fig. 2.4 shows the amplitude differentials of two different finger gestures. We can see that although the amplitude value of the first finger gesture is not obvious, the amplitude differential of the finger gesture is significantly different from that of white noises. Thus, we can utilize the amplitude differential for signal segmentation of finger gesture episodes. Specifically, *FingerPass* utilizes sliding windows to compare the amplitude differential with a predefined threshold for capturing the starting and ending point of a finger gesture. The threshold can be obtained through empirical studies.

2.3.3.2   Finger Gesture Recognition Based on SVM

Existing works on finger gesture recognition based on CSI of WiFi signals often utilize Dynamic Time Warping (DTW) as the recognition algorithm [7, 16]. However, the computational complexity of DTW-based recognition is typically on the order of $O(Knm)$ [11]. Here, K represents the number of known finger gestures, while n and m refer to the numbers of sampling points in the matching finger gesture episodes, respectively. Given this computational complexity, DTW-based recognition may not be able to meet the real-time requirement for finger gesture recognition. The complexity grows rapidly as the number of finger gestures and the length of the finger gesture episodes increase, making it challenging to achieve real-time performance.

To address the need for real-time response, *FingerPass* utilizes Support Vector Machine (SVM) for finger gesture recognition, combined with a one-versus-one strategy [15]. By constructing a multi-classifier, *FingerPass* achieves finger gesture recognition with a computational complexity of approximately $O(K^2 n)$. Here, K represents the number of finger gestures, and n denotes the number of sampling points in the finger gesture episodes. In practice, the number of finger gestures in a human-computer interaction system is typically limited. This leads to a significantly smaller value for K compared to the number of sampling points n. Therefore, the time consumption of the SVM-based method is considerably lower than that of DTW, enabling faster response times during human-computer interactions.

2.3.4 User Identification Through Deep Learning for Finger Gesture-Based Access Control

In smart homes, before a user interacts with smart household appliances, *FingerPass* should first obtain the identity credential in login stage. The user authentication in the login stage can be considered as an identification problem, i.e., identify the user by a specific login finger gesture, which is actually a multi-class problem.

The CSI phase of WiFi signals provides valuable information about the behavioral characteristics of each user during finger gestures. However, the presence of unconscious finger motions can introduce interference in the received CSI of WiFi signals. Given that finger gestures involve fine-grained movements, even subtle interference caused by unconscious motions can have a significant impact on the robustness of finger gesture-based user authentication. To ensure robust user identification, it is necessary to reduce the interference caused by these unconscious motions. A notable characteristic of finger gestures is the presence of a strong sequential relationship between the previous and subsequent finger motions. This sequential relationship provides a basis for distinguishing between the intentional finger gestures and the unintended unconscious motions. Unconscious motions during finger gestures differ from the normal sequential relationships observed in finger gestures. They induce instant significant shifts that are unrelated to the previous finger motions and do not affect the subsequent motions in a sequential manner. By leveraging the sequential relationships observed in finger gestures, we can extract unique features that capture the behavioral characteristics specific to each user.

Feature Extraction To utilize the sequential relationships in CSI phase induced by finger gestures, we propose a three-layer Long Short-term Memory-based Deep Neural Network (LSTM-based DNN) to extract features of each user's finger gestures for robust user identification. Figure 2.5 shows the architecture of user identification through the three-layer LSTM-based DNN.

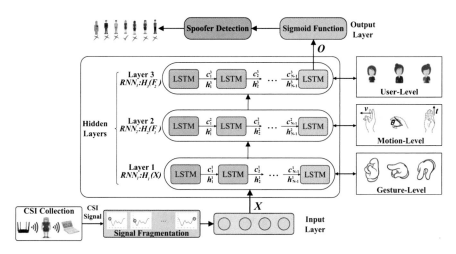

Fig. 2.5 Architecture of a three-layer LSTM-based deep neural network

In the proposed DNN model, each hidden layer is composed of a Recurrent Neural Network (RNN) with LSTM (Long Short-Term Memory) units. Traditional RNN models are limited in their ability to maintain long-term sequential relationships as they primarily focus on short-term previous information, which can result in the loss of important contextual dependencies that occurred in the distant past [2]. This hinders the comprehensive depiction of unique features from the behavioral characteristics of finger gestures. To capture both long-term and short-term information of finger gestures, LSTM units are employed instead of the typical neural units in RNN. LSTM units have been specifically designed to address the vanishing gradient problem and allow for the retention of long-term dependencies [5]. Within each hidden layer, an LSTM unit maps the input Z_t^l at time slot t and layer l to a feature representation f_t. This mapping is achieved through an activation function $g()$, a weight matrix P, and a bias b. The input Z_t^l comprises three components: $Z = [x_t^l, h_{t-1}^l, c_{t-1}^l]^T$. Here, x_t^l represents the current information, h_{t-1}^l represents the short-term information, and c_{t-1}^l represents the long-term information. By utilizing RNN with LSTM units, the model is able to retain both the long-term and short-term previous information of finger gestures. This enables the expression of more comprehensive sequential relationships and enhances the ability to robustly identify users based on their finger gesture patterns.

In the DNN model, each layer contains an RNN, denoted as H_i, which processes the input CSI phase profiles and produces a set of feature representations as output. The input CSI phase profiles of a user's finger gestures, denoted as X, are partitioned into N small fragments, represented as $x(t)$. This partitioning results in a sequence of fragmented CSI phase profiles: $X = [x(1), x(2), \ldots, x(N)]$, where $x(t)$ represents the fragmented CSI phase profiles at time slot t (with t ranging from 1 to N). In the DNN model, the inputs of the first layer are the fragmented CSI phase profiles X obtained from the user's finger gestures. The RNN in the first layer, $H_1(X)$, processes these inputs and extracts gesture-level features, denoted as F_1. The output F_1 from the first layer is then fed as input to the second layer. The RNN in the second layer, $H_2(F_1)$, further processes these features and extracts motion-level features, such as speed, angle, and time, denoted as F_2. Finally, the output F_2 from the second layer is passed to the last layer. The RNN in the last layer, $H_3(F_2)$, takes F_2 as input and extracts user-level features. These features, represented as an output O, capture the unique characteristics of the user and can be used for user identification purposes. By sequentially processing the input CSI phase profiles through the layers of the DNN model, the system effectively extracts gesture-level, motion-level, and user-level features, ultimately enabling robust user identification based on their finger gesture patterns.

User Identification In *FingerPass*, the Sigmoid function is employed in the output layer to identify a user's identity based on the extracted features. When a user attempts to log in, *FingerPass* calculates the posterior probability $P(U_k|O)$ using the output feature O of the user and the features of every registered user. This probability represents the likelihood that the current user is user U_k. For each registered user U_k, the posterior probability $P(U_k|O)$ is computed as

$$P(U_k \mid O) = \frac{P(O \mid U_k)P(U_k)}{P(O \mid U_k)P(U_k) + P(O \mid \overline{U}_k)P(\overline{U}_k)}. \tag{2.3}$$

Here, $P(U_k)$ is the prior probability of user U_k, and $P(O|U_k)$ represents the likelihood of feature O given the label U_k. The denominator in the equation ensures that the posterior probabilities satisfy the constraints $0 \leq P(U_k|O) \leq 1$ and $P(U_k|O) + P(\overline{U}_k|O) = 1$, where $\overline{U}_k$ denotes the complement of U_k. The Sigmoid function outputs K posterior probabilities, where K represents the number of user classes. The objective function, $k = \arg\max_{k \in K} P(U_k|O)$, determines the user with feature O and identifies them as user U_k. By comparing the posterior probabilities and selecting the user class with the highest probability, *FingerPass* accurately identifies the user based on their feature O.

Spoofer and Unexpected Body Movements Detection In addition to identifying the user's identity among multiple registered users, *FingerPass* incorporates spoofer detection during the login stage using the proposed DNN. Through the LSTM-based DNN, subtle differences between the finger gestures of a spoofer and those of all registered users can be extracted. These differences are utilized for spoofer detection. When a spoofer attempts to login using a finger gesture, their features are extracted by the LSTM-based DNN. Since the features of the spoofer would not match those of any registered user, the posterior probability of the spoofer in the output layer should be significantly lower than that of all registered users. This difference in probabilities is used to set a threshold for spoofer detection. Specifically, a similarity score, denoted as $score_k$, is defined as the similarity between the feature O of the attempted login finger gesture and the features U_k of all registered finger gestures. The score is defined as $score_k = 1$ if $P(U_k|O) > \lambda$, 0 if $P(U_k|O) \leq \lambda$. If the sum of the scores, $\sum_{k=1}^{K} score_k$, equals zero, it indicates that none of the registered user features match the attempted login user's feature O. In such a case, the attempted login user is identified as a spoofer. This approach is also effective in detecting unexpected body movements issued by the user. Since body movements are significantly different from valid finger gestures, the features extracted by the DNN would exhibit substantial dissimilarities. Even if an unexpected body movement is recognized as a finger gesture, *FingerPass* can further identify it as a spoofer's request and trigger no further permission or interaction response.

2.3.5 User Verification through SVDD for Finger Gesture-Based Interaction

In order to maintain continuous privacy protection and ensure consistent delivery of personalized services, *FingerPass* performs user authentication during each interaction involving finger gestures in the interaction stage. As discussed in Sect. 2.2.3, it is crucial to maintain real-time response to provide a satisfactory user experience. Consequently, user authentication in the interaction stage can be simplified to a verification problem, determining whether the current user is valid or invalid. This simplification essentially transforms the user authentication task into a binary classification problem. By simplifying user authentication to a binary classification problem, *FingerPass* focuses on differentiating between two categories: valid users and invalid users. This approach allows for efficient and real-time verification during interactions, ensuring the security and privacy of the system while maintaining a seamless user experience.

Verification Mechanism To ensure a real-time response, *FingerPass* employs a one-class classifier, Support Vector Domain Description (SVDD), to verify the identity of the current user. However, using SVDD based on a single finger gesture may result in lower classification accuracy due to its lightweight nature. To address this limitation and improve the authentication accuracy, *FingerPass* introduces a verification mechanism that leverages not only the current finger gesture interaction but also the previous finger gestures that have passed the verification during the ongoing interactions. The intuition behind this mechanism is that a user typically interacts with smart household appliances multiple times after successfully logging in. By considering the sequence of interactions, the verification mechanism gradually enhances the accuracy of the SVDD-based classifier. As the user performs successive interactions, the verification mechanism accumulates a history of verified finger gestures. This historical information is used to refine the SVDD-based classifier and adapt it to the user's unique behavioral characteristics. By incorporating the previous verified finger gestures into the verification process, *FingerPass* can continuously authenticate the user's identity for each interaction. This approach improves the accuracy of the SVDD-based classifier over time, leading to more reliable and robust user authentication.

During the training process of the SVDD-based classifier in *FingerPass*, the system trains not only single-gesture classifiers for individual finger gestures but also splices multiple finger gestures together to train multi-gesture classifiers. Specifically, we first align all CSI phases of finger gestures through the interpolation method to make the input's length consistent, and then feed the aligned relative phases into the classifier for training. Assume there are n finger gestures, i.e., $g_{(0)}, \ldots, g_{(n-1)}$, *FingerPass* trains finger gesture classifiers for single finger gesture and splicing finger gestures, i.e., for each finger gesture, *FingerPass* trains n single-gesture classifiers, $c_{g_{(0)}}, \ldots, c_{g_{(n-1)}}$; for the splicing of two gestures, *FingerPass* trains n^2 two-gesture classifiers, $c_{g_{(0)}g_{(0)}}, c_{g_{(0)}g_{(1)}}, \ldots, c_{g_{(0)}g_{(n)}}, c_{g_{(1)}g_{(0)}}, \ldots, c_{g_{(n-1)}g_{(n-1)}}$; $\ldots$; for the splicing of m finger gestures, *FingerPass* trains n^m m-gesture classifiers, $c_{g_{(0)}g_{(0)}\cdots g_{(0)}}, c_{g_{(0)}g_{(0)}\cdots g_{(1)}}, \ldots, c_{g_{(n-1)}g_{(n-1)}\cdots g_{(n-1)}}$. Through the training above, we can obtain $\sum_{i=1}^{m} n^i = \frac{n(1-n^m)}{1-n}$ classifiers including the single-gesture classifiers and the multi-gesture classifiers.

In the verification process, when a user performs the tth finger gesture interaction $g_{(t)}$, *FingerPass* utilizes classifiers of $m - 1$ previous finger gestures that passed the verification during the ongoing interactions combined with current finger gesture, i.e., $c_{g_{(t)}}, c_{g_{(t-1)}g_{(t)}}, \ldots, c_{g_{(t-m+1)}g_{(t-m+2)}\cdots g_{(t)}}$, to get m preliminary verification results. Then, *FingerPass* utilizes a voting mechanism that leverages the results of each classifier to obtain a final user verification result. Specifically, for each classifier, a user verification result $\mu_i \in \{1, 0\}$ is obtained, where $\mu_i = 1$ and $\mu_i = 0$ denote a successful and unsuccessful verifications respectively. Then, *FingerPass* votes on all the results, and decides the final user verification result according to the maximum voting results, i.e., $result = \{1 \mid \sum_{i=1}^{m} \mu_i > \frac{m}{2}, 0 \mid \sum_{i=1}^{m} \mu_i \leq \frac{m}{2}\}$, where $result = 1$ and $result = 0$ represent successful and unsuccessful verifications respectively. Similar to the unexpected body movement detection in the login stage, the interaction stage can also recognize an unexpected body movement as a spoofer's request, due to the significant difference between a valid finger gesture and the unexpected body movement.

The computational complexity of the SVDD-based classifier is $O(n)$, where n represents the size of each finger gesture sample. Considering the utilization of $m - 1$ previous finger gestures in our verification mechanism, the total number of classifiers applied is m. As a result, the computational complexity of user verification in the interaction stage is approximately $O(nm^2)$. To determine the optimal value of m, we conducted experiments using real-world data collected from various environments. The verification accuracy under different values of m is depicted in Fig. 2.6. When only a single gesture is used for user verification ($m = 1$), the verification accuracy is measured at 68.5%. However, as more previous finger gestures are incorporated into the verification process, the accuracy gradually improves. The highest accuracy of 89.2% is achieved when m is set to 3. Subsequently, the accuracy starts to decline due to overfitting. Considering that the optimal value of m is much smaller than n, the computational complexity of user verification in the interaction stage can be approximated as $O(n)$. This means that, through the SVDD-based verification mechanism with a small number of spliced

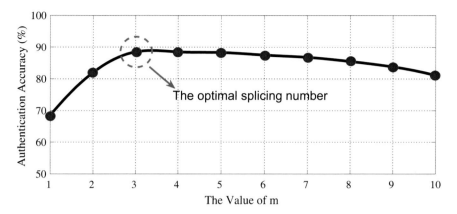

Fig. 2.6 Verification accuracy under different m

gestures, *FingerPass* achieves high user authentication accuracy while maintaining real-time response in the interaction stage.

2.4 Performance Evaluation

In this section, we evaluate the performance of *FingerPass* in real home environments.

2.4.1 Experimental Setup and Methodology

FingerPass is implemented on a HP Pavilion 14 laptop, which is equipped with an Intel WiFi Link 5300 NIC that provides 30 subcarriers on CSI of WiFi signals. For the experiments, a commercial wireless access point (AP), i.e., a TP-LINK-WDR5620, is used as the WiFi signal transmitter, continuously emitting WiFi signals. The experiments are conducted in three different home environments: a living room, a bedroom, and a kitchen. The sizes of these rooms are 5.8 × 4.2 m, 3.8 × 3.4 m, and 3.4 × 2.2 m, respectively. The distances between the AP and the laptop in these rooms are 3.0, 2.0, and 1.0 m, respectively. Figure 2.7 illustrates the layouts of the AP, laptop, and other furniture in the three home environments.

For our experiments, we select 8 commonly used finger gestures that are widely employed in human-computer interaction systems. These finger gestures are depicted in Fig. 2.8. A total of 7 volunteers participate in the experiments. Considering that the average number of individuals per family in the United States is approximately 3.14 [14], we designate 5 volunteers as registered users and the remaining 2 volunteers as spoofers. This setup reflects the typical composition of

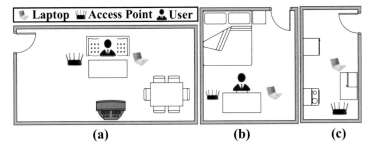

Fig. 2.7 Experimental setup of three home environments. (**a**) Living room. (**b**) Bedroom. (**c**) Kitchen

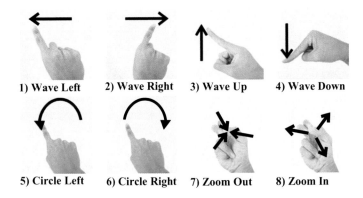

Fig. 2.8 Illustration of eight different finger gestures

most families. During the experiments, all volunteers are required to perform the finger gestures towards the laptop at a distance of 0.5m. This distance is chosen based on the natural positioning of users in front of the smart appliance, as users typically stand or sit in close proximity to the device during interactions.

We define several evaluation metrics:

- *Response Accuracy.* The probability that both the finger gesture and user's identity are recognized and authenticated correctly.
- *Response Time.* Assume the CSI of WiFi signals induced by a user's finger gesture is derived at time T_e, and the time that the system responds the user's interaction is T_{dev}. The response time of the system is defined as $T = T_{dev} - T_e$.
- *Confusion Matrix.* Each row and each column of the matrix denotes the ground truth and the authentication result of *FingerPass* respectively. The ith-row and jth-column entry of the matrix shows the percentage of samples that are authenticated as the jth user while actually are the ith user.
- *Authentication/Recognition Accuracy.* The probability that a user/finger gesture who is A is exactly identified as A.

- *False Accept Rate.* The probability that a user not a registered user is authenticated as a registered user.
- *False Reject Rate.* The probability that a user not a spoofer is authenticated as a spoofer.

2.4.2 Overall Performance

In Fig. 2.9a, the response accuracies of the login and interaction stages are presented. The average response accuracies for the login and interaction stages are found to be 91.3 and 88.6%, respectively. Consequently, the overall response accuracy of *FingerPass* is measured at 90.0%. These results demonstrate that *FingerPass* achieves satisfactory performance in both the interaction and authentication stages, ensuring reliable and accurate user authentication. Additionally, it can be observed that the response accuracies across the three different home environments are similar. This indicates that *FingerPass* exhibits robustness to varying distances between the transmitter and receiver, as well as different home environments.

Figure 2.9b shows the cumulative distribution functions (CDFs) of the response time in the login and interaction stages.The response time encompasses both finger gesture recognition and user authentication processes. It can be observed that in the interaction stage, approximately 85% of the finger gestures have response times of less than 200 ms. Conversely, in the login stage, the response times are in the range of 800–1200 ms. Previous research has established that response times ranging from 50 to 200 ms are considered appropriate for providing a satisfactory user experience in modern touch systems [9]. Since the login stage does not involve any interaction requests, the relatively longer response time in this stage does not significantly impact the user experience. In the interaction stage, *FingerPass* achieves a real-time response comparable to touch systems, meeting the criteria for delivering a seamless and enjoyable human-computer interaction experience.

2.4.3 Performance of User Authentication

Figure 2.10a shows the confusion matrix of *FingerPass* in the login stage. From the confusion matrix, it can be observed that *FingerPass* achieves an average authentication accuracy of 93.3% in identifying the registered users and an accuracy of 90.0% in spoofer detection. The average accuracy of the login stage in user authentication is 92.6%, with a standard deviation of 4.43%. These results indicate that *FingerPass* demonstrates a high level of accuracy in user authentication during the login stage.

Figure 2.10b shows authentication accuracies of *FingerPass* in the interaction stage under the three home environments. We can observe that *FingerPass* can achieve average authentication accuracies of 91.3, 89.8, and 89.2% under the three

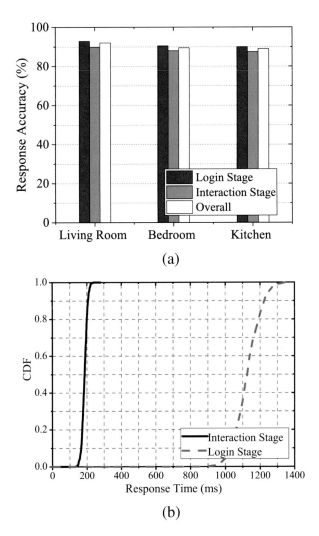

Fig. 2.9 Overall performance of *FingerPass*. (**a**) Response accuracy in different environments. (**b**) CDF of time in login and interaction stages

home environments respectively, and the standard derivations are 1.6, 1.7, and 1.3% respectively. This result indicates that *FingerPass* can accurately authenticate the logged-in user's identity in the interaction stage.

In Fig. 2.11, the false accept rates and false reject rates of *FingerPass* in the login stage are presented for different home environments. From the graph, it can be observed that the average false accept rate of *FingerPass* across the three environments is only 3.5%. This low false accept rate demonstrates the reliability of *FingerPass* in correctly identifying a spoofer during the login stage. Furthermore, the average false reject rate under the three home environments is measured at 3.8%.

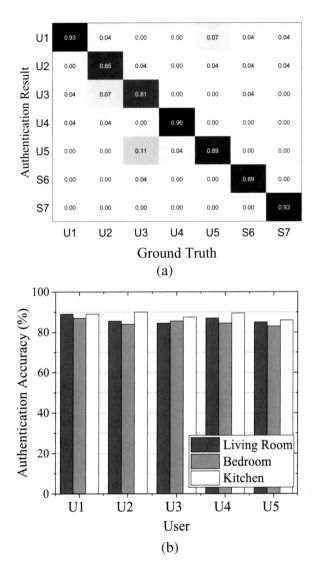

Fig. 2.10 Performance of user authentication in the login and interaction stages. (**a**) Confusion matrix of user authentication in login stage. (**b**) Authentication accuracy of *FingerPass* in interaction stage

This indicates that *FingerPass* rarely misidentifies a registered user during the login stage.

Figure 2.12 shows CDFs of interaction numbers for misidentifying a logged-in user and identifying a non-logged-in user in the interaction stage. It can be observed that over 90% of non-logged-in users can be authenticated within 3 interactions. This demonstrates that *FingerPass* is robust and not vulnerable to other users or

Fig. 2.11 False accept rate and false reject rate in login stage under different home environments

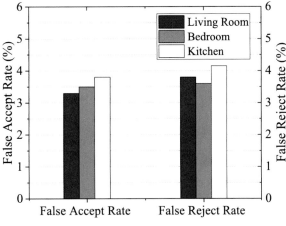

Fig. 2.12 CDFs of interaction numbers to misidentify a logged-in user and identify a non-logged-in user

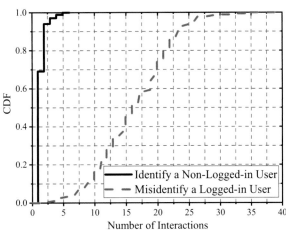

spoofers. Additionally, it can be observed that when the interaction numbers are below 10 times, approximately 90% of users are still not mistakenly logged out by *FingerPass*. This indicates that the continuous authentication mechanism employed by *FingerPass* rarely affects the normal use of the logged-in user.

2.4.4 Performance of Finger Gesture Recognition

To evaluate the performance of finger gesture recognition, we conducted a comparison between *FingerPass* and a baseline method based on Dynamic Time Warping (DTW) [7, 16]. Figure 2.13a presents the performance of *FingerPass* and the DTW-based method for different finger gestures. It can be observed that the average recognition accuracy of *FingerPass* is comparable to that of the DTW-

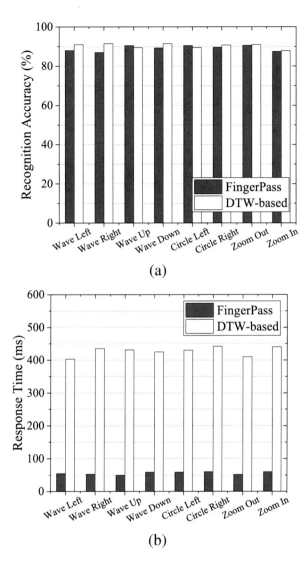

Fig. 2.13 Performance of finger gesture recognition for *FingerPass* and DTW-based method. (**a**) Recognition accuracy of the two methods. (**b**) Response time of the two methods

based method, achieving an average accuracy of 88.7%. This validates the reliability and effectiveness of *FingerPass* in accurately recognizing finger gestures, enabling seamless interaction between users and smart household appliances. Furthermore, Fig. 2.13b demonstrates the response time of *FingerPass* and the DTW-based method. The average response time of *FingerPass* is measured at 56.1 ms, meeting the real-time requirement for a satisfactory user experience. In contrast, the baseline method exhibits a response time above 350 ms, which exceeds the time range considered acceptable for a seamless user experience (i.e., 50–200 ms).

2.4.5   Performance Under Different Impacts

Impact of Training Set Size   In Fig. 2.14a, the impact of training set size on authentication accuracies in the login and interaction stages is examined for the three home environments. It can be observed that as the size of the training set increases, the authentication accuracies initially improve and then stabilize in both stages.

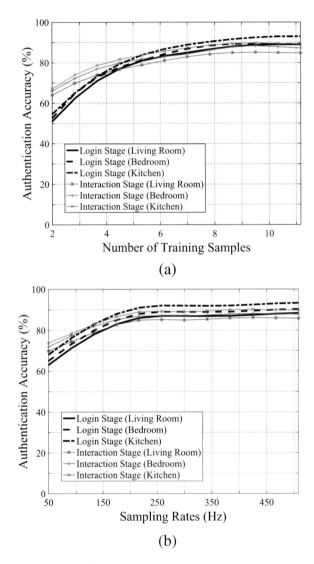

(a)

(b)

Fig. 2.14 Performance under different training sets and sampling rates. (**a**) Size of training sets. (**b**) Sampling rates

When users perform above 8 finger gestures for registering, *FingerPass* achieves average authentication accuracies of over 80% in both the login and interaction stages. This indicates that increasing the size of the training set beyond a certain point does not significantly contribute to improving authentication accuracy. A training set size of 8 finger gestures is deemed acceptable for users, as it leads to high authentication accuracies in both the login and interaction stages. This ensures that the register stage of *FingerPass* aligns well with user experiences, striking a balance between effectiveness and user convenience.

Impact of Sampling Rate   To investigate the impact of different sampling rates on the performance of *FingerPass*, we evaluated its authentication accuracy under various sampling rates. Figure 2.14b displays the authentication accuracy in the login and interaction stages for the three home environments. It can be observed that the authentication accuracy of *FingerPass* initially increases and then stabilizes as the sampling rate increases. When the sampling rate approaches 250 Hz, *FingerPass* achieves an authentication accuracy of over 85% in all three home environments. This indicates that *FingerPass* performs effectively with a sampling rate of around 250 Hz, which is suitable for most smart household appliances.

Impact of Distance Between User and Receiving Antennas   To evaluate the performance of *FingerPass* in comfortable interaction distances, we conducted experiments to explore its authentication accuracy at different distances between the user and the laptop. In smart home environments, the interaction distance between users and appliances varies depending on the type of appliance. For example, the average size of a smart TV in 2017 was 42.8 in, and the recommended viewing distance for the best viewing experience is below 1.6 m. This suggests that most appliances have interaction distances within 2.4 m that can meet the requirements for comfortable usage. In the experiments, the distance between the laptop and the AP was fixed at 1, 2, and 3 m in the three home environments. This allowed us to explore the performance of *FingerPass* within the specific distance range between the user and the laptop. From Fig. 2.15a, it can be observed that *FingerPass* achieves authentication accuracies of over 75% when the distance between the user and the laptop is less than 1.6 m in all three home environments. This demonstrates that *FingerPass* can achieve satisfactory performance for comfortable interactions within a typical distance range in smart home environments.

Impact of Ambient Persons   To evaluate the impact of an ambient person on the performance of *FingerPass*, we conducted experiments to study the authentication accuracy under different orientations of the ambient person relative to the laptop. The orientation of the ambient person is defined as the angle between the line connecting the AP and the laptop and the line connecting the AP and the ambient person. The orientation is measured counterclockwise relative to the AP-laptop connection, with 0 degrees representing the AP-laptop connection itself. In our experiments, the current user performed finger gestures at a distance of 0.5 m from the laptop, while the ambient person was positioned at a fixed distance of 0.5, 1, or 1.5 m from the laptop, depending on the environment. Figure 2.15b shows

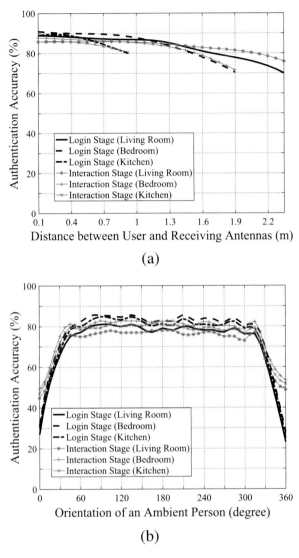

Fig. 2.15 Performance under different distance between user and antennas, and orientation of an ambient person. (**a**) Distance between user and antennas. (**b**) Orientation of an ambient person

the authentication accuracy of the login stage and the interaction stage under different orientations of the ambient person in the three home environments. From the results, it can be observed that the authentication accuracies remain stable and above 75% for orientations in the range of [40°, 320°], which indicates that *FingerPass* can achieve satisfactory performance when the ambient person is not positioned too close to the line-of-sight transmission of WiFi signals. However, the authentication accuracy significantly degrades for orientations in the range of

$[0°, 40°]$ and $[320°, 360°]$. This is due to the close distance between the ambient person and the line-of-sight WiFi transmission, which causes strong interference to the signal transmission.

2.5 Conclusion

In this chapter, we propose a finger gesture-based user authentication system, *FingerPass*, which leverages CSI of WiFi signals to continuously authenticate users during human-computer interactions. First, we pre-process and segment CSI of WiFi signals through amplitude differential, and then recognize finger gestures by Support Vector Machine. For highly accurate and real-time user authentication, *FingerPass* divides the whole authentication into two stages, i.e., login and interaction stages. For the login stage, we propose a deep learning-based approach, i.e., Long Short-Term Memory Deep Neural Network, for highly accurate user identification. For the interaction stage, to provide continuous user authentication in real time, a verification mechanism with lightweight classifiers is proposed to continuously authenticate the user during each interaction of finger gestures. Experiments show that *FingerPass* is reliable for continuous user authentication in smart homes.

References

1. Chen, B., Yenamandra, V., Srinivasan, K.: Tracking keystrokes using wireless signals. In: Proceedings of ACM MobiSys'15, Florence (2015)
2. Dorffner, G.: Neural networks for time series processing. In: Neural Network World. Citeseer (1996)
3. Gragnaniello, D., Poggi, G., Sansone, C., Verdoliva, L.: Local contrast phase descriptor for fingerprint liveness detection. Pattern Recognit. **48**(4), 1050–1058 (2015)
4. Halperin, D., Hu, W., Sheth, A., Wetherall, D.: Tool release: gathering 802.11 n traces with channel state information. ACM SIGCOMM Comput. Commun. Rev. **41**(1), 53–53 (2011)
5. Hochreiter, S., Schmidhuber, J.: Long short-term memory. Neural Comput. **9**(8), (1997)
6. Jin, Y., Soh, W.-S., Wong, W.-C.: Indoor localization with channel impulse response based fingerprint and nonparametric regression. IEEE Trans. Wireless Commun. **9**(3), 1120 (2010)
7. Li, H., Yang, W., Wang, J., Xu, Y., Huang, L.: Wifinger: talk to your smart devices with finger-grained gesture. In: Proceedings of ACM Ubicomp'16, Heidelberg (2016)
8. Market Research Community: Smart home automation market size, share and trends analysis. https://marketresearchcommunity.com/smart-home-automation-market
9. Ng, A., Lepinski, J., Wigdor, D., Sanders, S., Dietz, P.: Designing for low-latency direct-touch input. In: Proceedings of ACM UIST'12, Cambridge, pp. 453–464 (2012)
10. Ranjan, J., Whitehouse, K.: Object hallmarks: identifying object users using wearable wrist sensors. In: Proceedings of ACM Ubicomp'15, Osaka (2015)
11. Salvador, S., Chan, P.: Toward accurate dynamic time warping in linear time and space. Intell. Data Anal. **11**(5), 561–580 (2007)
12. Schroff, F., Kalenichenko, D., Philbin, J.: Facenet: a unified embedding for face recognition and clustering. In: Proceedings of IEEE CVPR'15, Boston, pp. 815–823 (2015)

13. Shi, C., Liu, J., Liu, H., Chen, Y.: Smart user authentication through actuation of daily activities leveraging wifi-enabled IoT. In: Proceedings of ACM MobiHoc'17, p. 5 (2017)
14. Statista: society-demographics-average size of a family in the us 1960–2017. https://www. statista.com/statistics/183657/average-size-of-a-family-in-the-us/
15. Suykens, J.A.K., Vandewalle, J.: Least squares support vector machine classifiers. Neural Process. Lett. **9**(3), 293–300 (1999)
16. Tan, S., Yang, J.: Wifinger: leveraging commodity wifi for fine-grained finger gesture recognition. In: Proceedings of ACM MobiHoc'16, Paderborn, pp. 201–210 (2016)
17. Wang, W., Liu, A.X., Shahzad, M., Ling, K., Lu, S.: Understanding and modeling of wifi signal based human activity recognition. In: Proceedingso of ACM MobiCom'15, New York (2015)
18. Wu, J., Konrad, J., Ishwar, P.: Dynamic time warping for gesture-based user identification and authentication with kinect. In: Proceedings of IEEE ICASSP'13, Vancouver (2013)
19. Zeng, Y., Pathak, P.H., Mohapatra, P.: Wiwho: wifi-based person identification in smart spaces. In: Proceedings of IEEE IPSN'16, Vienna, p. 4 (2016)
20. Zhang, L., Tan, S., Yang, J., Chen, Y.: Voicelive: a phoneme localization based liveness detection for voice authentication on smartphones. In: Proceedings of ACM CCS'16, Vienna, pp. 1080–1091 (2016)
21. Zhuo, Y., Zhu, H., Xue, H., Chang, S.: Perceiving accurate csi phases with commodity wifi devices. In: Proceedings of IEEE InfoCom'17 (2017)

Chapter 3
Gesture-Independent User Authentication Using WiFi

Abstract User authentication is an essential mechanism to support various secure accesses. Although recent studies have shown initial success on authenticating users with human activities or gestures using WiFi, they rely on predefined body gestures and perform poorly when meeting undefined body gestures. This chapter aims to enable WiFi-based user authentication with undefined body gestures rather than only predefined body gestures, i.e., realizing a gesture-independent user authentication. In this chapter, we first explore physiological characteristics underlying body gestures, and find that statistical distributions under WiFi signals induced by body gestures can exhibit invariant individual uniqueness. Inspired by this observation, we propose a user authentication system *FreeAuth*, which utilizes WiFi signals to identify individuals in a gesture-independent manner. Specifically, we design an adversarial learning-based model, which suppresses specific gesture characteristics, and extracts invariant individual uniqueness unrelated to specific body gestures, to authenticate users in a gesture-independent manner. Extensive experiments in indoor environments show that the proposed system is feasible and effective in gesture-independent user authentication.

Keywords User authentication · Gesture independence · WiFi signals · Adversarial learning

3.1 Introduction

In recent years, there has been a significant increase in the use of user authentication across various infrastructures, including typical, mobile, and IoT devices. This surge aims to safeguard user privacy and ensure the security of sensitive information. Traditional authentication methods primarily rely on knowledge factors such as passwords and PINs, or on inherent biometric traits like fingerprints and facial features. However, these approaches often require additional interactions that can interrupt ongoing operations. A more recent trend in user authentication is behavior-based authentication, which involves verifying a person's identity based on their everyday activities or gestures. This approach has gained considerable attention due to its ability to strike a balance between security requirements and nonintrusive user experiences. For instance, it enables legitimate users to access private information seamlessly while engaging in their regular activities, while simultaneously preventing unauthorized users from maliciously accessing confidential documents.

In the pursuit of user authentication using human daily activities or gestures, certain studies [6, 9] have utilized wearable devices to extract behavioral features from users. However, this approach requires active involvement from users and incurs additional costs. In an effort to achieve non-intrusive authentication, other research [13, 15] has explored vision-based methods for behavior-based authentication. However, these approaches face similar challenges as other visual applications, such as being sensitive to lighting conditions and raising privacy concerns. To overcome these challenges, recent studies [4, 7, 10, 11] have focused on leveraging widely-available WiFi signals to sense specific daily activities or gestures for authentication. This approach offers potential solutions that are less dependent on user involvement and do not incur additional costs. Additionally, it addresses concerns related to lighting conditions and privacy.

However, these approaches rely on predefined activities and gestures, i.e., they must be previously learned in the registration process. In practical scenarios, if user authentication can be carried out in any body gestures (i.e., activities and gestures), it is able to support security protections for a wide range of real-world situations. For instance, in an IoT environment with heightened security requirements, a safety guard should be able to authenticate a user whenever they perform any arbitrary body gesture, including daily activities or human-computer interactions. This would provide real-time secure access to the IoT environment. To achieve this goal, our objective is to develop a user authentication system that not only supports predefined body gestures but also caters to undefined body gestures, ultimately realizing gesture-independent user authentication. Due to the wide deployment of WiFi infrastructures and the contact-free manner of WiFi-based sensing, we consider leveraging WiFi signals to achieve user authentication. To realize such an authentication system, we face several challenges in practice. First, we need to extract fine-grained features caused by human body gestures from commodity WiFi signals. Second, we need to characterize the invariant individual uniqueness that is in depth embedded underlying various body gestures. Finally, we should accurately identify individuals without the restriction of predefined body gestures.

In this chapter, we first delve into the nature of human body gestures, and observe that inherent physiological characteristics significantly influence these gestures, resulting in invariant individual uniqueness across different body gestures. This observation implies that there are distinct physiological traits underlying various gestures. To extract this invariant individual uniqueness, we exploit the statistical distributions present in the Channel State Information (CSI) of WiFi signals induced by body gestures, and find different individuals exhibit individual differences in these statistical distributions across a range of body gestures. We propose a gesture-independent user authentication system *FreeAuth*, which eliminates the need for predefined gestures. *FreeAuth* first utilizes Convolutional Neural Network (CNN) to extract fine-grained features induced by body gestures. Then,

FreeAuth employs Recurrent Neural Network (RNN) to extract specific gesture characteristics, which aims to suppress behavioral interferences of body gestures. Meanwhile, *FreeAuth* uses Gaussian Mixture Model (GMM) to characterize individual uniqueness through statistical distributions, which aims to enhance the capability of extracting unique physiological characteristics. Through optimizing the two opposed objectives with adversarial learning, i.e., *FreeAuth* can identify individuals in a gesture-independent manner. Our experiments validate the effectiveness of gesture-independent user authentication.

The rest of the chapter is organized as follows. Section 3.2 presents the preliminary analysis. Section 3.3 gives the system design of *FreeAuth*. Then, we evaluate the system and present the results in Sect. 3.4. Finally, we give our conclusion in Sect. 3.5

3.2 Preliminary

In this section, we present the insight of invariant individual uniqueness underlying body gestures, and then explore the feasibility of leveraging WiFi signals to extract invariant individual uniqueness for gesture-independent authentication.

3.2.1 Insight of Invariant Individual Uniqueness Underlying Body Gestures

To gain insight into the invariant individual uniqueness underlying body gestures, we begin by analyzing the generative process of a body gesture. Typically, a body gesture involves the movement of a person's limbs and torso, customized to suit their unique physiology. Consequently, human body gestures are inherently constrained by individual physiological characteristics, such as limb length and the power generated by limb movements. These physiological attributes play a crucial role in determining the behavioral uniqueness of different individuals. For instance, people with varying muscle masses exhibit distinct accelerations and velocities when performing gestures, resulting in their individual behavioral uniqueness. Therefore, it is the specific physiological characteristics of each person that give rise to their behavioral uniqueness. An existing study [8] further supports the notion that human body gestures are shaped by these inborn physiological characteristics. This finding motivates us to extract the unique physiological attributes that underlie body gestures for the purpose of authentication.

Intrinsic physiological characteristics differ from extrinsic behavioral characteristics in that they are gesture-independent. These features remain constant for an individual, irrespective of the type of body gesture being performed. Physiological characteristics are more closely associated with the inherent physical and biochemical functions of individuals, as described in studies of human physiology [14]. As a result, these features exhibit minimal variation across different body gestures, thus contributing to the invariant individual uniqueness. Motivated by this understanding, our goal is to explore the feasibility of extracting and utilizing unique physiological characteristics for user authentication.

3.2.2 Feasibility Study of Gesture-Independent Individual Identification Using WiFi

To investigate the feasibility of gesture-independent user authentication, we conduct an experiment to extract unique physiological characteristics underlying body gestures using WiFi signals. We leverage Channel State Information (CSI) of WiFi signals, which provides detailed information about the channel properties and propagation paths, allowing for fine-grained sensing of human movement [2]. In the experiment, two participants perform three different body gestures: turning on a light, fetching a cup, and plugging in a power adapter. We used a laptop equipped with an Intel WiFi Link 5300 NIC and three external receive antennas to capture the WiFi signals during the experiment. Figure 3.1 illustrates the normalized relative CSI phase induced by a body gesture for the two users. The relative CSI phase is obtained by comparing the CSI from consecutive antennas. From Fig. 3.1, we can observe that the signal patterns of the two users are distinct even when they perform the same body gesture. These differences stem from the unique behavioral characteristics and individuality of each user. Similarly, the other two body gestures also exhibit unique signal patterns induced by the users' behavioral uniqueness.

However, Directly observing individual differences of physiological characteristics underlying body gestures from CSI of WiFi signals is challenging. To extract the unique physiological characteristics for gesture-independent authentication, we take inspiration from text-independent speaker verification techniques [1] and focus on modeling the underlying statistical distributions of physiological observations. We disregard the temporal sequences of CSI and instead model the statistical distributions to capture the invariant uniqueness of each individual. Principle Component Analysis (PCA) method is applied to reveal the correlations between different CSI sequences and highlights principal components that minimize redundancy. This allows us to uncover the statistical distributions present in the CSI sequences. Figure 3.2 showcases the distributions of two principal components obtained from CSI induced by two users performing the three different gestures. The x-axis represents the first dominant component derived from PCA, indicating the primary movement information for each gesture. The y-axis represents a carefully selected component of the PCA results. We can observe that the three different body gestures are distinctly separated, demonstrating the accurate gesture recognition capability of WiFi signals. Furthermore, from another perspective shown in Fig. 3.2b, we can observe that even when performing different body gestures, the two users remain

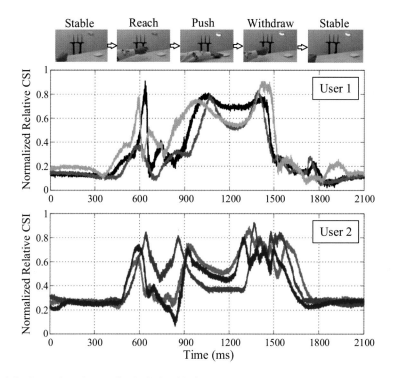

Fig. 3.1 Illustration of normalized relative CSI for two users

distinguishable to some extent. This observation suggests the presence of invariant individual uniqueness within the statistical distributions underlying the CSI induced by body gestures.

3.3 System Design

In this section, we present the design details of the gesture-independent user authentication system, *FreeAuth*.

3.3.1 System Overview

Figure 3.3 shows the system architecture, which is divided into a model construction stage and a user authentication stage.

In the model construction stage, *FreeAuth* requires users to perform several body gestures, and employs WiFi signals to sense the body gestures as training data

Fig. 3.2 Distributions of the three gestures performed by the two users in two principal components. (**a**) Distinguish body gestures. (**b**) Distinguish users

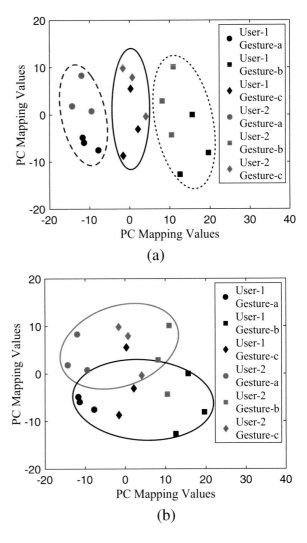

(a)

(b)

for one-off model construction. *FreeAuth* first preprocesses the received signals through calculating relative CSI, and then segments the signals into episodes of each body gesture based on the changing rate of relative CSI. Then, *FreeAuth* constructs an adversarial neural network, including a Convolutional Neural Network (CNN)-based feature extractor, a Recurrent Neural Network (RNN)-based gesture suppressor, and a Gaussian Mixture Model (GMM)-based user authenticator. In the adversarial neural network, the feature extractor extracts fine-grained features from the input signals, and the features are fed into the gesture suppressor and user authenticator respectively. After that, the gesture suppressor extracts specific gesture characteristics, while the user authenticator characterizes individual uniqueness unrelated to specific body gestures. Through training the neural network in an

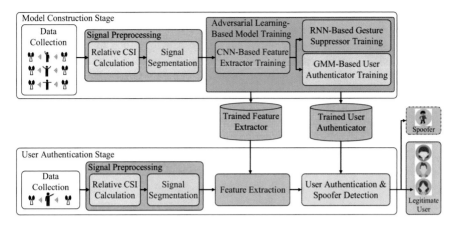

Fig. 3.3 System architecture of *FreeAuth*

adversarial learning way, *FreeAuth* finally obtains a trained feature extractor which can extract features independent of specific body gestures, and a trained user authenticator which is able to identify individuals through the extracted features.

In the user authentication stage, *FreeAuth* authenticates a user based on the body gestures performed the user. *FreeAuth* first preprocesses and segments the CSI of received WiFi signals induced by the user's body gestures, which is the same as that in the model construction stage. Then, *FreeAuth* uses the trained feature extractor to extract features from the body gesture performed by the user, and further applies the trained user authenticator to identify the user.

3.3.2   Signal Preprocessing

FreeAuth first preprocesses raw CSI by calculating relative CSI and segmenting body gesture sequences.

Relative CSI Calculation Commodity WiFi operates at a frequency that corresponds to a centimeter-level wavelength (e.g., 5.17 cm for the 5.8 GHz band), making it capable of capturing movement at a similar scale. However, the presence of errors in raw CSI data hampers its direct use for human movement sensing. To mitigate these errors, we employ relative CSI, which is calculated by performing conjugate multiplication between the CSI values obtained from two adjacent antennas in the same receiver. This approach is based on the assumption that while different WiFi cards may not be time-synchronized, all transceiver chains on a single WiFi card share the same sampling clock, resulting in the same hardware errors [5]. By leveraging relative CSI, we can effectively reduce the impact of errors and enhance the accuracy of movement sensing. Furthermore, to address low-frequency (e.g., < 5 Hz) and high-frequency (e.g., > 100 Hz) noises, we apply a Butterworth filter to the received CSI. The filter's passband is set between 5 and 100 Hz, which covers the frequency range associated with most body gestures [11]. By eliminating noises outside this frequency range, we can further enhance the reliability and accuracy of the sensing system.

Signal Segmentation   To effectively extract features from body gestures, *FreeAuth* segments consecutive signal series into episodes of each independent body gesture. Since the errors in CSI relative phase are eliminated through conjugate multiplication, the variance of relative phase only results from human movement. Hence, to separate each body gesture from adjacent ones in a consecutive signal series, we propose to detect variance of relative phase and compare the variance with a threshold for signal segmentation. The variance of relative phase is calculated by the difference between adjacent elements. However, in practice, some variances within a body gesture are also below the threshold. Figure 3.4a shows the variances of two

Fig. 3.4 Illustration of signal segmentation. (**a**) Normalized relative phase and variances for continuous gestures. (**b**) Accuracy of signal segmentation under different settings

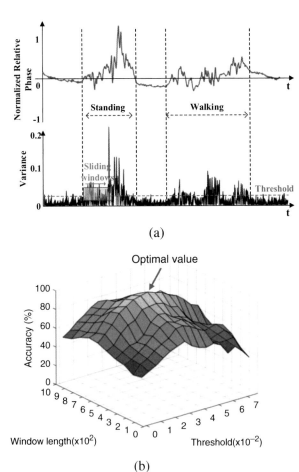

body gestures, i.e., standing up and walking. We can observe that some variances in walking are below the threshold, which may result in a false segmentation and discard useful behavioral information. To accurately segment body gestures, we employ sliding windows to measure the overall variance condition within each time window. Specifically, if half of the variances are above the threshold, the signal in the sliding window is considered as the component of a body gesture, and the first point higher than the threshold is judged as the start of the body gesture. On the contrary, half of the variances lower than the threshold is considered as interval, which the last point higher than the threshold is judged as the end of the body gesture. The length of sliding windows and the value of threshold are empirically studied. Figure 3.4b shows the gesture segmentation accuracy under different threshold values and window lengths. It can be observed that there is a trade-off between threshold and window length, where segmentation accuracy could reach 99.4% with a threshold of 0.04 and window length of 600. Hence, through sliding windows with the empirically studied parameters, *FreeAuth* effectively segments signals into episodes of each body gesture.

3.3.3   Adversarial Learning-Based Model Construction

To address the presence of both gesture characteristics and underlying physiological characteristics in the CSI of WiFi signals induced by body gestures, we propose an adversarial learning-based authentication model. Specifically, we employ adversarial neural network [3] to effectively suppress the behavioral interference caused by body gestures and extract the invariant individual uniqueness that is unrelated to specific gestures.

3.3.3.1   Designing the Adversarial Neural Network for Gesture-Independent Authentication

Figure 3.5 shows the architecture of the adversarial neural network designed for gesture-independent authentication.

Feature Extractor   The feature extractor extracts fine-grained features from CSI of WiFi signals induced by body gestures to characterize individual uniqueness (i.e., physiological characteristics of each individual). The input of feature extractor is the preprocessed CSI of WiFi signals. In order to make full use of the CSI of all communication links and all subcarriers, *FreeAuth* reshapes the received CSI under t communication links and m subcarriers in each communication link to $(m \cdot t) \times n$-dimension, where n is the length of each segmented relative CSI amplitude or phase. Then, *FreeAuth* integrates the relative CSI amplitude and phase as a two-channel input I with $2 \times (m \cdot t) \times n$-dimension, which embeds non-linear features induced by body gestures. Since the Convolutional Neural Network (CNN), especially the

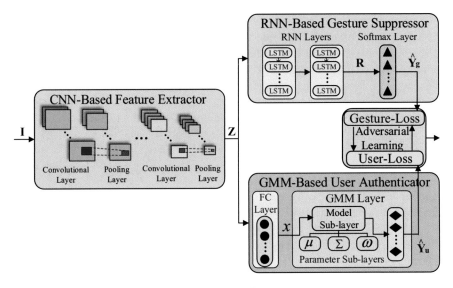

Fig. 3.5 Architecture of the adversarial neural network

convolutional operation, is specialized in well abstracting non-linear features, we select it as the basis of feature extractor.

The proposed CNN-based feature extractor consists of six layers, i.e., three convolutional layers and three pooling layers. The convolutional layer abstracts the input I as a compressed representation through the convolutional operation, and the pooling layer further reduces the dimension of the compressed representation. Specifically, the input I is first fed to the first convolutional layer with 32 convolutional kernels of 5×5-dimension to derive a compressed feature map. After that, the compressed feature map is normalized by the batch normalization operation, and further activated by a Rectified Linear Unit (ReLU) function for accelerating the convergence velocity during model training. Then, the activated feature map is further fed to the first max pooling layer of 2×2-dimension to reduce the feature dimension. By analogy, the reduced feature map is fed to the second convolutional and pooling layers, as well as the third convolutional and pooling layers in turn. The second and third convolutional layers are with $64\ 4 \times 4$-dimension and $128\ 3 \times 3$-dimension convolutional kernels respectively. Both convolutional layers are normalized with the batch normalization and activated by the ReLU function. Also, the second and third pooling layers both conduct the max pooling operation of 2×2-dimension. Through the stack of the 6 layers, the feature extractor finally extracts a feature map Z, which is further fed to the gesture suppressor and user authenticator respectively.

Gesture Suppressor Since the fine-grained features are extracted from the CSI induced by body gestures, specific gesture characteristics are inevitably contained underlying the extracted features. Hence, we need to suppress the behavioral interferences of body gestures to extract features independent of specific body gestures. We thus develop a gesture suppressor to suppress the behavioral interferences of body gestures. The behavioral interferences of body gestures are embedded underlying the sequential relationship of input representations, which depict the content of body gestures. Therefore, we employ the Recurrent Neural Network (RNN) that explores the sequential relationship in the inputs to construct the gesture suppressor.

The gesture suppressor consists of two RNN layers with Long Short-Term Memory (LSTM) units and a softmax layer. Specifically, the gesture suppressor first partitions the feature map Z from the feature extractor into N small fragments, i.e., $Z = [Z_1, Z_2, \ldots, Z_N]$. Then, the fragmented inputs Z are fed to the two stacked RNN layers with LSTM units successively. Based on the two RNN layers, feature R is extracted as the output to represent the sequential relationships of body gestures underlying the extracted feature Z. The output R is further activated by the softmax layer to derive the probability $\hat{Y}_g$ which represents the probability of recognizing body gestures, i.e.,

$$\hat{Y}_g = softmax(W_g R + b_g), \tag{3.1}$$

where W_g and b_g are the weight and bias respectively, and $\hat{Y}_g = \{\hat{Y}_g^1, \cdots, \hat{Y}_g^n\}$. The probability is under the constraints that $0 \leqslant \hat{Y}_g^k \leqslant 1$ and $\sum_{k=1}^n \hat{Y}_g^k = 1$. This probability serves as the basis of gesture-loss for model construction, which aims to suppress the behavior interferences of body gestures.

User Authenticator As mentioned in Sect. 3.2.2, the physiological characteristics exist in statistical distributions underlying the CSI induced by body gestures. Inspired by text-independent speaker identification [1], we employ Gaussian Mixture Model (GMM) to construct a user authenticator to identify individuals in a gesture-independent manner. GMM can utilize multiple Gaussian distributions to fit the statistical distributions of an arbitrary input, which indicates that the statistical distributions of CSI can be extracted from GMM to characterize physiological characteristics for gesture-independent authentication.

The GMM-based user authenticator consists of a Fully Connected layer (i.e., FC layer) and a GMM layer [12]. In the fully connected layer, the feature map Z is first linearly combined with the weight W_1 and bias b_1, and then activated by Rectified Linear Unit (ReLU) function to derive an intermediate representation x, i.e., $x = ReLU(W_1 Z + b_1)$. Afterwards, the intermediate representation x is further fed into the GMM layer. The GMM layer consists of a model sub-layer to fit the statistical distributions of input features, three parameter sub-layers to store relative parameters, and an output sub-layer to calculate identity probability. In particular, assume there are n users registering in the system. The model sub-layer thus contains n nodes, each of which employs a GMM model to fit the distributions of each registered user under input features. Each node s (which corresponds to a registered user) is a likelihood function, which consists of g Gaussian functions, i.e.,

$$p(x|s) = \sum_{i=1}^{g} \omega_{si} \mathcal{N}(x, \mu_{si}, \Sigma_{si}), \tag{3.2}$$

where $\mathcal{N}(x, \mu_{si}, \Sigma_{si})$ is the ith Gaussian function for node s, ω_{si}, μ_{si} and Σ_{si} are the weight, mean and covariance for the ith Gaussian function respectively. To support the model sub-layer, the three additional parameter sub-layers store the weights $\omega_s = [\omega_{s1}, \cdots, \omega_{sg}]$, means $\mu_s = [\mu_{s1}, \cdots, \mu_{sg}]$, and covariances $\Sigma_s = [\Sigma_{s1}, \cdots, \Sigma_{sg}]$ for all the nodes s ($s \in [1, \cdots, n]$) of the model sub-layer, respectively. After calculating the likelihoods, the GMM layer further derives the logarithm joint distribution in the output layer, i.e.,

$$\log(p(x, s)) = \log(p(s)) + \log(p(x|s)), \tag{3.3}$$

where $p(s)$ is the prior of each registered user. The posterior probability $p(s|x)$ thus can be derived as

$$p(s|x) = \frac{p(x, s)}{\sum_s p(x, s)}. \tag{3.4}$$

Based on the posterior probabilities, the GMM-based user authenticator finally derives the user identity probability $\hat{Y}_u = \{\hat{Y}_u^1, \cdots, \hat{Y}_u^n\}$, where $\hat{Y}_u^s = p(s|x), s \in [1, n]$. The probability is under the constraints that $0 \leqslant \hat{Y}_u^s \leqslant 1$ and $\sum_{s=1}^{n} \hat{Y}_u^s = 1$. This probability servers as the basis of user-loss for model construction, which aims to enhance the capability of extracting individual uniqueness.

3.3.3.2 Training the Authentication Model Based on Adversarial Learning

Although the three sub-networks has seemingly collaborative function, the authentication model can achieve gesture independence only when they collaborate effectively. *FreeAuth* trains the authentication model through adversarial learning for gesture-independent authentication.

To train the authentication model, *FreeAuth* first initializes the structure and parameters of the designed adversarial neural network. Since the number for registered users only determines the structure of GMM layer, we initial the structure of the GMM layer by configuring it with n nodes same with the number of registered users. Then, we initialize the parameters of the neural network. The weights and biases of the CNN-based feature extractor are initialized as random values from normal distribution and a constant of 0.1 respectively. The weights and bias of the RNN-based gesture suppressor are initialized as orthogonal matrices (which are derived from singular value decomposition of a normal distribution matrix) and a constant of 0.1 respectively to avoid gradient vanishing and explosion. For the

GMM-based user authenticator, the μ-layer and Σ-layer are set as random values from normal distribution and unit matrices respectively, and the ω-layer is initialized with uniform values of $1/g$.

After initialization, the adversarial neural network is then trained to enable gesture-independent authentication based on adversarial learning. Given the input I, the feature extractor abstracts a feature map Z. Then, the feature map Z is fed to the gesture suppressor and user authenticator to derive gesture probability vector $\hat{Y}_g$ and user identity probability vector $\hat{Y}_u$ respectively. After that, we derive gesture-loss and user-loss from the two kinds of probabilities. Specifically, given the identified identity probability vector $\hat{Y}_u$ from the user authenticator and the ground truth Y_u, the user-loss is defined as:

$$L_u = -\sum_{i=0}^{|U|-1} Y_u^i \log(\hat{Y}_u^i), \tag{3.5}$$

where Y_u^i and $\hat{Y}_u^i$ are the ith entries in the corresponding probability vectors, and $|U|$ is the length of the two probability vectors determined by the number of registered users. Similarly, given the recognized gesture probability vector $\hat{Y}_g$ and the encoded gesture probability vector of ground truth Y_g, the gesture-loss is defined as:

$$L_g = -\sum_{k=0}^{|G|-1} Y_g^k \log(\hat{Y}_g^k), \tag{3.6}$$

where Y_g^k and $\hat{Y}_g^k$ are the kth entries in the corresponding probability vectors, and $|G|$ is the length of the two probability vectors determined by the number of gesture kinds in the training data.

With the two loss functions (i.e., Eqs. (3.5) and (3.6)), *FreeAuth* can be optimized to extract gesture-independent individual uniqueness through maximizing the gesture-loss while minimizing the user-loss. However, since the specific gesture characteristics are more significant than the underlying physiological characteristics in the initial inputs, the optimization objective at the beginning of model training needs to lay emphasis on suppressing the behavioral interferences of body gestures. With the gradual optimization of suppressing behavioral interferences, the model training should turn to focus on characterizing invariant individual uniqueness for a gesture-independent authentication. Hence, linear combination of the two losses with subtract operations cannot balance the above optimization priority. Based on the analysis above, we employ a non-linear function (i.e., the exponential function) to combine the gesture-loss and user-loss, i.e.,

$$\min L = \min(\alpha(L_u + b) + \beta e^{-L_g + c}), \tag{3.7}$$

where α and β are weights of the user-loss and gesture-loss respectively, and b and c are the biases for user-loss and gesture-loss respectively. The non-linear function takes advantage of the property of the exponential function to gradually lower the priority of suppressing behavioral interferences of body gestures, and thereby relatively raises the priority of characterizing individual uniqueness with the gradual optimization. Using the combined optimization objective above, the adversarial neural network-based authentication model can be gradually trained with the capability of extracting invariant individual uniqueness from the feature extractor, and identifying individuals through the extracted individual uniqueness from the user authenticator.

3.4 Evaluation

In this section, we evaluate the system performance of *FreeAuth* in indoor environments.

3.4.1 Experimental Setup and Methodology

To extract the CSI of WiFi signals, we utilize laptops equipped with Intel WiFi Link 5300 NIC and the Linux 802.11n CSI Tool [2]. These laptops serve as WiFi transmitters and receivers in our experimental setup. The WiFi transmitter continuously emits WiFi signals at a frequency of 5 GHz with a sampling rate of 2000 samples per second. The two WiFi receivers, each equipped with external antennas, capture the WiFi signals and extract the CSI using the Linux 802.11n CSI Tool. The distance between adjacent antennas is set to half the wavelength of the WiFi signal. To evaluate the performance of the *FreeAuth* system under various environmental conditions, we conduct the experiment in three indoor environments: a meeting room, a laboratory, and an apartment. Figure 3.6 illustrates the layout of these three environments. During the experiment, users are asked to perform body gestures within the rectangular region formed by the WiFi transmitter and receivers. The sensing area has dimensions of 2×2 m, providing sufficient coverage for capturing the WiFi signals induced by the body gestures. To capture ground truth for body gestures and user identities, a camera is placed in each environment to continuously record videos.

For the experiment, we recruit a total of 30 volunteers, consisting of 18 males and 12 females. The age of the participants ranges from 21 to 45 years old. The participants are divided into two groups: the legitimate user group and the spoofer group. Each group consists of 9 males and 6 females, ensuring a balanced gender distribution. The age distributions of the two groups are also similar. The legitimate users register on *FreeAuth* through performing body gestures, and the spoofers attempt to deceive the system.

To ensure the reliability and fairness of the experiment, we adopt a five-fold cross-validation approach. This approach mitigates the impact of subjective gesture

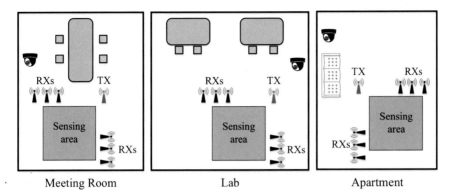

Fig. 3.6 Experimental environments

Table 3.1 Body gestures and corresponding groups

Group 1	Stand up, turn on the light, pick up the phone, type keyboard
Group 2	Walk, wear the coat, open the door, clean the desk
Group 3	Sit down, throw the rubbish, hang out the cloth, wear glasses
Group 4	Turn around, pick up a cup, plug the power adapter, sweep the floor
Group 5	Open the drawer, take off the hat, pick up the tableware, turn the book

selection and enables comprehensive evaluation using different combinations of the 20 gestures. The 20 gestures are divided into 5 groups, with each group containing 4 gestures. The grouping is shown in Table 3.1. During each round of cross-validation, 4 groups of gestures are designated as "known gestures" for model training. This means that each legitimate user provides data for training by performing these 16 known gestures. The remaining group of gestures is treated as "unknown gestures" and is not used for training but only for evaluation purposes. By performing 5 rounds of cross-validation, we obtain a comprehensive evaluation of *FreeAuth*. During each cross-validation round, legitimate users are required to perform each known gesture 12 times to train the authentication model. For evaluation purposes, each user performs each body gesture 15 times, including both the known and unknown gestures. Finally, we obtain final evaluation performance by averaging the 5 cross validations.

3.4.2 Overall Performance

Figure 3.7 shows the confusion matrices for legitimate user identification for known and unknown gestures. The confusion matrix exhibits which legitimate identity or not a legitimate identity (i.e., an empty identity represented by 'E') is identified for each user. In the case of known gestures, *FreeAuth* achieves an overall authentication accuracy of 91.3% with a deviation of 2.1% in identifying legitimate

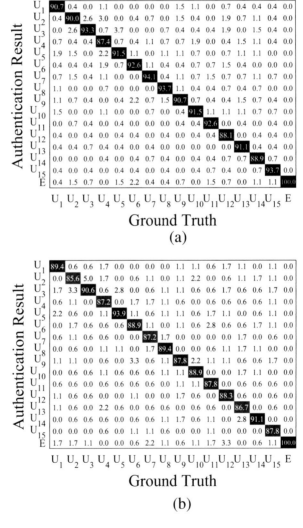

Fig. 3.7 Confusion matrices of authentication accuracy under known and unknown gestures. (**a**) Known gestures. (**b**) Unknown gestures

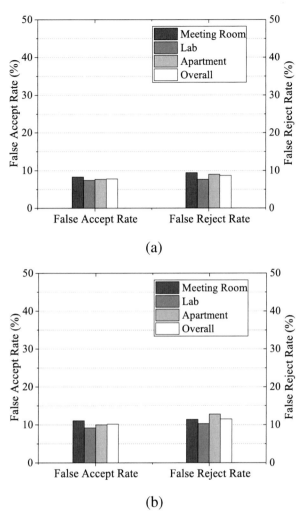

Fig. 3.8 FAR and FRR for unknown gestures. (**a**) Known gestures. (**b**) Unknown gestures

users. This result indicates that *FreeAuth* performs satisfactorily in traditional user authentication scenarios, where known gestures are used. For unknown gestures, *FreeAuth* achieves an overall authentication accuracy of 88.5% with a deviation of 2.4% in identifying legitimate users. The difference in authentication accuracies between known and unknown gestures is only 2.8%, which is relatively small. These results demonstrate the effectiveness of *FreeAuth* in identifying users in a gesture-independent manner.

Figure 3.8a, b show the FAR and FRR under known and unknown gestures in the three environments. It can be observed that for known gestures, *FreeAuth* achieves an overall FAR of 7.8% and FRR of 8.7%. As for unknown gestures, *FreeAuth* achieves overall FAR and FRR of 10.1% and 11.5% respectively, which are only slightly higher than that of known gestures. This result further demonstrates that *FreeAuth* can authenticate users in the gesture-independent manner. Also, we observe that the accuracy deviation among different environments is not significant, i.e., only 0.9% in average. This result indicates that *FreeAuth* is robust in authenticating users under different indoor environments with various room sizes and layouts.

3.4.3 Comparison with Baseline Approaches

By authenticating users in the gesture-independent manner, *FreeAuth* enables more general and flexible authentication capability compared with existing gesture-dependent approaches. We further evaluate the effectiveness of our system on user authentication by comparing with 3 state-of-the-art gesture-dependent approaches, i.e., *Smart* [11], *WiID* [10], and *FingerPass*, which act as the baseline for comparison. For variable control, the process of training and evaluation for the three approaches follows the guideline of *FreeAuth* described in the evaluation setup, so all the four approaches are with the same training data and evaluation methodology.

Figure 3.9 shows the authentication performance of the four approaches under known and unknown gestures respectively. For known gestures, we can see that the three baseline approaches achieve over 92% accuracy, and *FreeAuth* achieves a similar authentication accuracy of 90.7%, which demonstrates an effective traditional authentication capability of the proposed system. On the other hand, for unknown gestures, the three baseline approaches suffer from significant performance decline for about 30% compared with *FreeAuth*. This is because the existing approaches do not involve gesture-independent techniques to their systems. Moreover, we can see that the deviation of authentication accuracies of *FreeAuth* is smaller than

Fig. 3.9 Authentication accuracy of different approaches

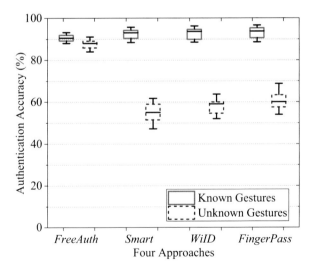

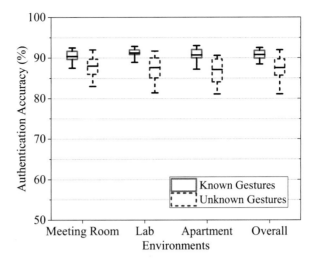

Fig. 3.10 Authentication accuracy under cross validations

other approaches. This is because the adversarial learning can avoid the impact of different gestures on model training, and *FreeAuth* extracts more generalized features from different gestures to enable robust user authentication. The above result demonstrates the improvement of *FreeAuth* over baseline approaches.

3.4.4 Robustness Performance

To evaluate the robustness performance of *FreeAuth* under different gesture sets, we analyze the authentication accuracy among different rounds of cross validation. Since the cross validation mechanism conducts several rounds of evaluation where different combinations of gesture sets are used as training and testing samples, the deviation among different validation rounds is able to exhibit the robustness of *FreeAuth* among different gesture sets. Figure 3.10 shows the authentication accuracy among the cross validations in three environments with known and unknown gestures. It can be first observed that the differences between different environments are insignificant, which is consistent with previous results. Besides, the performances among cross validations for the known gestures are more stable than that of unknown gestures. Specifically, the deviation of authentication accuracies under known gestures for cross validations is only 2.06%, while that under unknown gestures is 6.13%. This result indicates that different gesture sets could affect the authentication performance under unknown gestures.

Fig. 3.11 Authentication
accuracy with different loss
functions

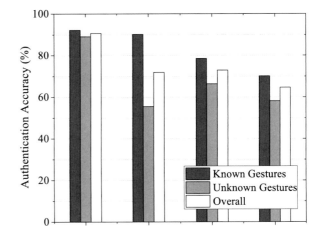

3.4.5 *Impact of Loss Function*

Loss function is a key design of the adversarial neural network in *FreeAuth*. In
this experiment, in addition to the exponential function combining the user-loss
and gesture-loss (i.e., $L = $ Eq. (3.7)), we employ three other loss functions,
i.e., only user-loss function ($L_1 = \alpha_1 L_u$), linear function for loss combination
($L_2 = \alpha_2 L_u + \beta_2(-L_g) + c_2$), and logarithmic function for loss combination
($L_3 = \alpha_3 L_u + \beta_3 \log(-L_g + c_3)$).

Figure 3.11 shows the authentication accuracy of *FreeAuth* with the four different
loss functions. It can be observed that *FreeAuth* with the loss function L has the best
authentication performance among all proposed loss functions. For other three loss
functions, the authentication accuracies under unknown gestures decrease below
70%. This is because L_1 only minimizes the user-loss without suppressing the
body gesture interferences, which lefts abundant gesture-specific information in
the extracted features. The linear function L_2 takes both user-loss and gesture-
loss into consideration, but the simple linear combination of the two losses cannot
well balance the priority of interference suppression and uniqueness extraction.
As for the logarithmic function L_3, it optimizes the model following to gradually
strengthen the suppression of gesture interferences, and thereby occupies the priority of extracting individual uniqueness, which is not an appropriate optimization
way to extract the gesture-independent features.

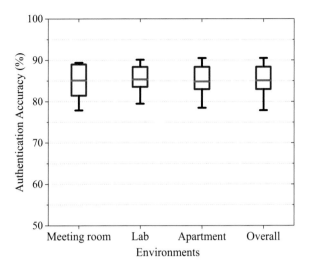

Fig. 3.12 Authentication accuracy for in-the-wild evaluation

3.4.6 In-the-Wild Evaluation

Since *FreeAuth* aims to realize gesture-independent user authentication, the evaluation that releases the restriction of performing specific gestures can comprehensively evaluate the system performance. Hence, we conduct an in-the-wild evaluation where users perform body gestures without any gesture kind restriction, to mirror the reality of actual gesture-independent authentication scenarios.

Figure 3.12 shows the authentication accuracy of in-the-wild experiment. We can see from the figure that the mean authentication accuracies are 85.1, 85.4, and 84.8% for the three environments respectively, which demonstrates an insignificant impact of environment layout. The overall authentication accuracy of in-the-wild experiment is 85.1%. Compared with the overall authentication accuracy (i.e., 89.9%) for all designed gestures, the authentication accuracy of in-the-wild scenario does not decline much. This result indicates that our system can achieve an acceptable performance for practical gesture-independent authentication. However, it can be also observed that the variances among different users are significant. For example, in the apartment, the best authentication performance for a user is 90.5% while the worst is only 78.5%. By analyzing the behavior contents of these users from the video, we conclude that the user who performs more complex and conspicuous body gestures tends to be identified more precisely. This is because these gestures provide more information about behavioral and physiological characteristics of the individual.

3.4.7 *Impact of Training Data Size*

The training data size depends on the number of samples for each body gesture, and the number of body gesture kinds for training. A large training data size requires frequent performing of body gestures during registration, while a small training data size could not support the model with sufficient generalization ability.

We first evaluate the performance of *FreeAuth* under different numbers of samples for each body gesture. Figure 3.13a shows authentication accuracies with

Fig. 3.13 Authentication accuracy under different training sizes. (**a**) Sample number of each gesture. (**b**) Number of gesture kinds

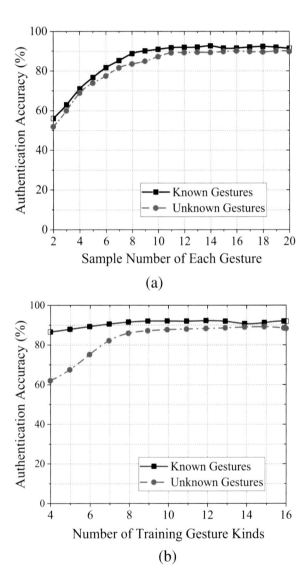

different numbers of samples for each gesture in model training under known and unknown gestures respectively. We can see that as the number of samples for each gesture increases, the authentication accuracies first increase rapidly, and then go stable. When the number of samples for each gesture increases to 12, *FreeAuth* could achieve around 91 and 88% authentication accuracies under known and unknown gestures respectively. More training samples would not contribute to an improvement in system performance.

We also evaluate the performance of *FreeAuth* under different numbers of body gesture kinds. In this experiment, we involve 12 samples for each body gesture, which follows the results of the previous experiment. The numbers of gesture kinds for testing under known and unknown gestures are both set as 4 for variable control of the experiment. Figure 3.13b shows the authentication accuracy of *FreeAuth* under different numbers of body gesture kinds in model training under known and unknown gestures. It can be observed from the figure that under known gestures, the authentication accuracy remains stable at around 90% as the number of body gesture kinds increases. But for unknown gestures, the authentication accuracy first increases rapidly and then tends to be stable with the increase of body gesture kinds. This is because as the number of body gesture kinds increases, *FreeAuth* is capable with rich prior knowledge of physiological characteristics from various body gestures, which helps to improve the capability of *FreeAuth* on gesture-independent user authentication. It can be also observed that as the number of body gesture kinds increases to 10 for model training, *FreeAuth* approaches 90% authentication accuracy for both known and unknown gestures. Such a number of body gesture kinds during registration is acceptable for most users.

3.5   Conclusion

In this chapter, we propose a user authentication system, *FreeAuth*, which leverages WiFi signals to identify individuals in a gesture-independent manner. First, we explore the physiological characteristics underlying body gestures, and find that different individuals exhibit individual differences in the statistical distributions under WiFi signals induced by various body gestures. We propose an adversarial learning-based model, which can suppress the behavioral interferences of body gestures, and extract invariant individual uniqueness unrelated to specific body gestures. With the model, *FreeAuth* can continuously identify individuals through arbitrary body gestures. Experiment results in real indoor environments demonstrate that *FreeAuth* is effective in gesture-independent user authentication.

References

1. Gish, H., Schmidt, M.: Text-independent speaker identification. IEEE Signal Process. Mag. **11**(4), 18–32 (1994)
2. Halperin, D., Hu, W., Sheth, A., Wetherall, D.: Tool release: gathering 802.11 n traces with channel state information. ACM SIGCOMM Comput. Commun. Rev. **41**(1), 53–53 (2011)
3. Jiang, W., Miao, C., Ma, F., Yao, S., Wang, Y., Yuan, Y., Xue, H., Song, C., Ma, X., Koutsonikolas, D., et al.: Towards environment independent device free human activity recognition. In: Procedings of ACM MobiCom'18, New Delhi, pp. 289–304 (2018)
4. Kong, H., Lu, L., Yu, J., Chen, Y., Tang, F.: Continuous authentication through finger gesture interaction for smart homes using wifi. IEEE Trans. Mobile Comput. **20**, 3148–3162 (2020)
5. Kotaru, M., Joshi, K., Bharadia, D., Katti, S.: Spotfi: decimeter level localization using wifi. In: Proceedings of ACM SIGCOMM'15, London, pp. 269–282 (2015)
6. Li, Y., Xie, M.: Understanding secure and usable gestures for realtime motion based authentication. In: Proceedings of IEEE INFOCOM WKSHPS'18, Honolulu, pp. 13–20 (2018)
7. Li, C., Liu, M., Cao, Z.: Wihf: enable user identified gesture recognition with wifi. In: IEEE INFOCOM'20, Toronto, pp. 586–595. IEEE, Piscataway (2020)
8. Mjaaland, B.B., Bours, P., Gligoroski, D.: Walk the walk: attacking gait biometrics by imitation. In: Proceedings of ISC'10, pp. 361–380 (2010)
9. Ranjan, J., Whitehouse, K.: Object hallmarks: identifying object users using wearable wrist sensors. In: Proceedings of ACM Ubicomp'15, Osaka (2015)
10. Shahzad, M., Zhang, S.: Augmenting user identification with wifi based gesture recognition. Proc. ACM Interact. Mob. Wearable Ubiquitous Technol. **2**(3), 134 (2018)
11. Shi, C., Liu, J., Liu, H., Chen, Y.: Smart user authentication through actuation of daily activities leveraging wifi-enabled IoT. In: Proceedings of ACM MobiHoc'17, Chennai, p. 5 (2017)
12. Variani, E., McDermott, E., Heigold, G.: A Gaussian mixture model layer jointly optimized with discriminative features within a deep neural network architecture. In: Proceedings IEEE ICASSP'15, South Brisbane, pp. 4270–4274 (2015)
13. Wang, X., Tanaka, J.: Gesid: 3d gesture authentication based on depth camera and one-class classification. Sensors **18**(10), 3265 (2018)
14. Wikipedia: Physiology (2019). https://https://en.wikipedia.org/wiki/Physiology/
15. Wu, J., Konrad, J., Ishwar, P.: Dynamic time warping for gesture-based user identification and authentication with kinect. In: Proceedings of IEEE ICASSP'13, Vancouver (2013)

Chapter 4
Multi-User Authentication Using WiFi

Abstract Existing works utilize WiFi signals to capture a user's activities for non-intrusive and device-free user authentication, but multi-user authentication remains a challenging task. In this chapter, we present a multi-user authentication system, *MultiAuth*, which can authenticate multiple users with a single commodity WiFi device. The key idea is to profile multipath components of WiFi signals induced by multiple users, and construct individual CSI from the multipath components to solely characterize each user for user authentication. Specifically, we propose a MUltipath Time-of-Arrival measurement algorithm (MUTA) to profile multipath components of WiFi signals in high resolution. Then, after aggregating and separating the multipath components related to users, *MultiAuth* constructs individual CSI based on the multipath components to solely characterize each user. To identify users, *MultiAuth* further extracts user behavior profiles based on the individual CSI of each user through time-frequency analysis, and leverages a dual-task neural network for robust user authentication. Extensive experiments involving 3 simultaneously present users demonstrate that *MultiAuth* is accurate and reliable for multi-user authentication with 87.6% average accuracy and 8.8% average false accept rate.

Keywords WiFi signals · Multi-user authentication · Multipath profiling · Individual CSI construction

4.1 Introduction

In recent times, there has been a significant push to expand the Internet of Things (IoT) into a broader concept known as the Internet of Everything (IoE) [4]. Rather than solely connecting things like mobile devices online, the IoE aims to integrate humans, processes, data, and things, connecting everything to the cyber world. As a result, user authentication, which forms the foundation for mapping humans to the cyber world, becomes crucial for both security guarantees and diverse IoE applications. In contrast to conventional authentication methods like passwords, fingerprints, and face recognition, user authentication for IoE requires

J. Yu et al., *WiFi signal-based user authentication*, SpringerBriefs in Computer Science, https://doi.org/10.1007/978-981-99-5914-3_4

more advanced capabilities. These include the ability to authenticate users without additional interaction and the capacity to authenticate multiple users simultaneously. Meeting these demands for IoE applications has sparked numerous research endeavors focused on achieving user authentication with these advanced capabilities.

To achieve authentication without additional interaction, several existing studies have utilized WiFi signals to sense daily activities for user authentication [2, 6, 7, 12, 14]. However, these WiFi-based approaches are primarily designed for single-user scenarios and have limited applicability in supporting a broader range of multi-user scenarios. In order to cater to the widely deployed multi-user collaboration scenarios, it becomes necessary to authenticate multiple users simultaneously without requiring extra interaction. For instance, in the enterprise domain, smart factories can associate workers and their activities with their identities, enabling the tracing of previous activities and facilitating the prompt execution of current activities for collaborative intelligent manufacturing. Similarly, in the realm of entertainment, the entertainment system can link real-world players and their activities to virtual-world identities, thereby supporting motion sensing games that involve multiple players.

Utilizing the omnidirectional propagation and multipath effect of WiFi signals, it is possible to leverage the Channel State Information (CSI) to capture the activities of multiple users and enable user authentication in multi-user scenarios. Our objective is to achieve multi-user authentication by analyzing human daily activities using WiFi signals. To implement multi-user authentication using WiFi signals, we face several challenges in practice. First, we should accurately profile the multipath components of WiFi signals to capture each user's activity individually under multi-user scenarios. Second, we need to use only single WiFi device to distinguish multiple users. Third, we should extract robust behavioral features from each user to enable multi-user authentication.

In this chapter, we propose a multi-user authentication system, *MultiAuth*, which authenticates multiple users simultaneously with single commodity WiFi device. The key idea is to profile multipath components of WiFi signals induced by multiple users, and construct individual CSI from the multipath components to solely characterize each user for user authentication. Specifically, we first present a MUltipath Time-of-Arrival measurement algorithm (MUTA) to measure the Time-of-Arrival (ToA) of signal propagation paths for multipath profiling in high resolution. Then, after aggregating and separating users' multipath components, we construct individual CSI of each user to solely characterize a user. Next, we conduct time-frequency analysis on individual CSI to obtain user behavior profiles, and design a Convolutional Neural Network-Recurrent Neural Network (CNN-RNN)-based dual-task model to extract fine-grained features from the profiles for robust user authentication. Extensive experiments demonstrate that *MultiAuth* could simultaneously authenticate up to 3 users with average 87.6% authentication accuracy and 8.8% false accept rate.

The rest of the chapter is organized as follows. In Sect. 4.2, we give a preliminary analysis of the system. Section 4.3 presents the design overview of *MultiAuth*. Sect. 4.4 describes the detailed design. Then, we conduct extensive experiments and present the results in Sect. 4.5. The chapter ends with a conclusion in Sect. 4.6.

4.2 Preliminary

To realize multi-user authentication using WiFi signals, we first present our observations on multipath profiling for multi-user authentication. Then, we propose a high-resolution ToA estimation method, and further study the feasibility of multi-user authentication using WiFi signals.

4.2.1 Theoretical Fundamental of Multipath Profiling Using CSI

To identify and authenticate multiple users leveraging WiFi signals, a potential solution is to profile the signal components reflected by different users and extract each user's behavioral features from the corresponding signal components. Since WiFi signals reflected by users who are located at different positions propagate with different path lengths, we can estimate propagation delays (i.e., Time-of-Arrival, ToA) of multipath components in WiFi signals and thereby separate the signals induced by multiple users.

As a well-known and mature ToA estimation solution, Inverse Fast Fourier Transform (IFFT) computes channel impulse response on CSI of WiFi signals and estimates propagation delays of different paths [9, 13]. The time resolution of IFFT depends on signal bandwidth [13], i.e., $\Delta = 1/B$, where Δ is the time resolution and B is the bandwidth. Due to a narrow bandwidth in commodity WiFi, it is usually challenging to separate multipath components accurately using IFFT. For example, a bandwidth of 200 MHz can be achieved in commodity 5.8 GHz WiFi by channel splicing [13], which leads to a time resolution of 5 ns and space resolution of 1.5 m with the IFFT approach. This indicates that the paths within 1.5 m in space are merged as one path. Hence, it is difficult to utilize IFFT to solve multi-user authentication problems where multiple users may exist closely in an indoor environment.

4.2.2 High Resolution ToA Estimation Using MUTA

To estimate the ToA of WiFi signals in high resolution for multi-user authentication, different from IFFT, we propose a MUltipath Time of Arrival estimation algorithm (MUTA). The algorithm is developed from MUltiple SIgnal Classification algorithm (MUSIC) [5], which is a classic Angle-of-Arrivals (AoAs) estimation method through the phase shift across antennas. We observe that the relationship between AoAs and signals received at different antennas is analogous to the relationship between ToAs and signals received at different subcarriers. Inspired by the observation, we propose MUTA to estimate multipath ToAs through phase shifts across subcarriers for high-resolution multipath profiling.

The rationale that supports MUTA is as follows. The phase shifts across subcarriers are closely associated with ToAs. Also, the phase shifts across subcarriers introduced by different ToAs are linearly independent, i.e., $h_i(f_2)/h_i(f_1) = e^{-j2\pi(f_2-f_1)\Delta t_i}$, where $h_i(f_2)$ and $h_i(f_1)$ are the i-th path's CSI with respect to two subcarriers f_2 and f_1, and Δt_i is i-th path's ToA. According to a theory in spatial spectrum estimation [5], applying eigenspace decomposition on the covariance matrix of signals could derive eigenvectors corresponding to a zero eigenvalue, and the eigenvectors are orthogonal to a matrix that steers the propagation of signals, such as angel and time. For example, the covariance matrix of signals measured across antennas can be decomposed into eigenvectors that are orthogonal to a steering matrix about AoAs, which is the basic idea of MUSIC. Accordingly, once we arrange the signals with linearly independent phase shifts in subcarriers to a matrix and its covariance matrix can derive eigenvectors with eigenvalue zero, we can analogously derive ToAs. Based on the basic idea, we design MUTA, which is a novel solution to estimate ToAs of multipath components. In MUTA, we first construct a steering matrix that describes phase shifts across subcarriers with respect to ToAs. Then, we construct a measurement matrix corresponding to CSI measurements, and finally search peaks in a pseudo-spectrum to estimate ToAs of multipath components.

Constructing Steering Matrix A steering matrix describes the relation between phase shifts and the parameters that need to be estimated (i.e., ToA). Suppose WiFi signals are transmitted from a transmitter and propagate through D paths with different lengths to arrive at a receiver, as shown in the left of Fig. 4.1. For Orthogonal Frequency-Division Multiplexing (OFDM)-based WiFi signals that propagate with multiple subcarriers, one path's phase shift introduced at m-th subcarrier relative to the first subcarrier is $-2\pi(m-1)f_\delta\Delta t$, where f_δ is the frequency difference between adjacent subcarriers, and Δt is the ToA of the path,

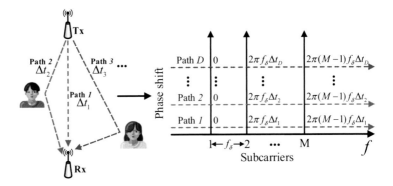

Fig. 4.1 ToA measurement with CSI phase shifts

as illustrated in the right part of Fig. 4.1. For simplicity, we denote the complex exponential of these phase shifts as a function of ToA, so the phase shifts in complex exponential across all M subcarriers can be denoted by a vector $a(\Delta t) = \left[1 \ e^{-j2\pi f_\delta \Delta t} \ \cdots \ e^{-j2\pi(M-1)f_\delta \Delta t}\right]^T$, which is also known as a steering vector. Based on the phase shifts of each path, we construct a steering matrix that describes the phase shifts for all D paths, i.e., $A = [a(\Delta t_1), a(\Delta t_2), \cdots, a(\Delta t_D)]$.

Constructing Measurement Matrix Based on the CSI measurement of WiFi signals, we further construct a measurement matrix. The received signal X that contains the CSI measurement with multiple subcarriers can be denoted as

$$X = \begin{bmatrix} h(f_1) & h(f_2) & \cdots & h(f_W) \\ h(f_{W+1}) & h(f_{W+2}) & \cdots & h(f_{2W}) \\ \vdots & \vdots & \cdots & \vdots \\ h(f_{(L-1)W+1}) & h(f_{(L-1)W+2}) & \cdots & h(f_{LW}) \end{bmatrix}, \tag{4.1}$$

where $h(f_i)$ is the CSI value of the i-th subcarrier, L is the maximal number of multipath components, W is the number of samples to estimate each path, and $L \times W$ equals the number of available subcarriers. To balance the trade-off between multipath resolving and noise resistance, we set L and W equal for each CSI measurement. This matrix of received signal is also known as the measurement matrix.

In wireless communications, the process of signal propagation can be described by a data model [10], i.e., $X = AS + N$. In the equation, S is the transmitted signal denoted by

$$S = \begin{bmatrix} h_1(f_1) & h_1(f_2) & \cdots & h_1(f_W) \\ h_2(f_1) & h_2(f_2) & \cdots & h_2(f_W) \\ \vdots & \vdots & \cdots & \vdots \\ h_D(f_1) & h_D(f_2) & \cdots & h_D(f_W) \end{bmatrix}, \tag{4.2}$$

where $h_i(f_j)$ denotes the CSI of the i-th multipath component under j-th subcarrier. A is the steering matrix, and $N = \left[N_1 \ N_2 \ \cdots \ N_D\right]^T$ is noise. ToAs in the steering matrix can be further estimated from the relation between measurement matrix and steering matrix.

Searching in Pseudo-Spectrum Based on the spatial spectrum estimation theory [5] and the data model [10], MUTA can estimate ToAs as long as the steering matrix A is derived from the measurement matrix. We first perform eigenvalue decomposition of the covariance matrix $R = XX^H$, where X^H is the conjugate transpose of X. Then, D eigenvectors of the largest D eigenvalues are selected to form a signal subspace. The remaining $M - D$ eigenvectors form a noise subspace U_N. Since the noise subspace is orthogonal to the steering matrix of signals [5],

ToAs are estimated in a pseudo-spectrum $P_{MU}(\Delta t)$, i.e.,

$$P_{MU}(\Delta t) = \frac{1}{a^T(\Delta t)U_N U_N^H a(\Delta t)}. \tag{4.3}$$

The ToA Δ_t of a path shows a maximum value in the pseudo-spectrum, which can be detected by searching peaks in P_{MU}. Therefore, by estimating the ToAs of signals, the proposed MUTA resolves the WiFi signals to multiple paths, each of which propagates with different delays.

Resolution Analysis The theoretical resolution of MUTA can be derived according to the resolution analysis of MUSIC, through the analogy between ToA and AoA, space (i.e., the parameter corresponds to antennas) and frequency (i.e., the parameter corresponds to subcarriers). Based on a universal analysis model of MUSIC-based AoA estimation [15], we develop the relationship between the threshold of Signal-Noise-Rate (SNR_t) and time resolution Δ_t as

$$SNR_t = 360(\frac{m-2}{mW})(\pi m \Delta f \Delta_t)^{-4}, \tag{4.4}$$

where m and W are the dimension and column of measurement matrix, $\Delta f = 312.5\,kHz$ is the frequency difference between two subcarriers. Take the 5 GHz commodity WiFi as an illustration. Overall 200 MHz bandwidth signals can be spliced as a whole according to [13], which provides 560 subcarriers available to form a measurement matrix with $m = 560$ and $W = 24$. The SNR threshold of WiFi signals can be set as 10 dB [1]. Under the setting, MUTA improves time resolution from 5.0 to 2.0 ns and space resolution from 1.5 to 0.6 m compared to IFFT. Therefore, applying MUTA promotes the resolution of multipath profiling of WiFi signals, which can be utilized for multi-user authentication.

4.2.3 Feasibility Study for Multi-User Authentication Using CSI

To achieve multi-user authentication, we further explore the feasibility of authenticating multiple users based on the multipath components measured by MUTA. We first collect CSI of WiFi signals in a static environment, and employ MUTA to calculate the pseudo-spectrum P_{MU} for each CSI packet. The result of pseudo-spectrum is shown in Fig. 4.2a. It can be observed that there are several multipath components indicating the line-of-sight signals and static reflected signals, each of which keeps stable across CSI packets. Then, we further collect CSI of WiFi signals from two users walking simultaneously in the same environment. As shown in Fig. 4.2b, the ToAs of specific multipath components in the pseudo-spectrum change dynamically with the two users' movement. This indicates that users'

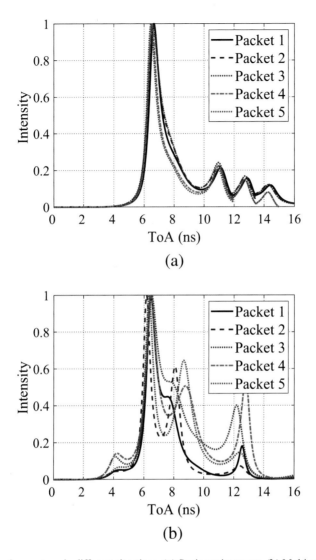

Fig. 4.2 Pseudo-spectrum in different situations. (**a**) Static environment. (**b**) Multi-user walking

movements affect the multipath length, which is consistent with the theoretical analysis of MUTA. Furthermore, we remove the multipath components stable among ToA by calculating the differential between CSI packets to explicitly exhibit users' movements, as shown in Fig. 4.3a. It can be observed that there remain two significant peaks, representing the multipath components reflected by the two users respectively. The result demonstrates that the proposed MUTA is able to resolve the multipath components induced by multiple individuals.

Fig. 4.3 Pseudo spectrum of two users and corresponding statistical distribution. (**a**) Pseudo-spectrum for 5 CSI packets after static removing. (**b**) Statistical distribution of different users' activities

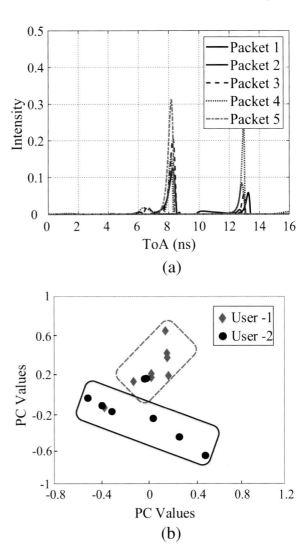

Afterward, we further explore multi-user authentication based on multipath components of WiFi signals. The change of a path's ToA, i.e., the shift of a peak's position in the pseudo-spectrum, indicates the length change of the path, which is relevant to the motion amplitude of users. Thus, change of ToA is roughly applied to distinguish users in this section. To extract individual uniqueness, we explore statistical distribution for different users to explore differences among individuals. Specifically, we calculate the first-order difference of a path's ToAs over time for each movement, which is a one-dimensional vector (i.e., each element in the vector is the path's ToA difference between two adjacent packets). Since Principal Component Analysis (PCA) could enlarge the variance between different samples to exhibit dominated statistical distribution, we employ PCA on the vectors collected from several times of movement by the two users. Figure 4.3b shows the statistical distribution of these samples using PCA. It can be observed that most of the samples are aggregated in two regions, which demonstrates that the two users could be roughly distinguished through the multipath components induced by human movement. With the encouraging results, we are motivated to exploit rich information underlying multipath components of WiFi signals for multi-user authentication.

4.3 Design Overview

In this section, we present the threat model and system overview for the multi-user authentication system *MultiAuth*.

4.3.1 Threat Model

In the threat model, our system considers the possibility of one or more spoofers attempting to deceive the authentication system, thereby gaining unauthorized access to multi-user collaboration applications. These spoofers aim to deceive the system by assuming the identity of one of the legitimate users. To detect and prevent such attacks, *MultiAuth* uses WiFi signals to sense the activities of all users. By analyzing the sensed activities of each user individually, the system can identify and differentiate between legitimate users and potential spoofers. The threat model can be further refined into two distinct types of attacks: zero-effort attacks and imitation attacks. In a zero-effort attack, the spoofer attempts to deceive the system without any prior knowledge about the behaviors of the legitimate users. In an imitation attack, the spoofer seeks to deceive the system by specifically imitating the behaviors of one of the legitimate users.

4.3.2 System Overview

Figure 4.4 shows the architecture of *MultiAuth*, which includes two stages, i.e., the register stage and authentication stage.

In the register stage, each user performs specific activities multiple times, such as walking or standing up. The system collects Channel State Information (CSI) of WiFi signals affected by the user's activities and utilizes the MUltipath Time of Arrival measurement algorithm (MUTA) to perform multipath profiling. By aggregating the multipath components associated with the user, individual CSI profiles are constructed to characterize each user uniquely. Based on the user

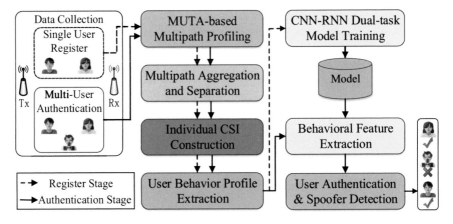

Fig. 4.4 System overview of *MultiAuth*

behavior profiles derived from the individual CSI, *MultiAuth* trains a Convolutional Neural Network-Recurrent Neural Network (CNN-RNN)-based dual-task model to extract features relevant to authentication. Once all users have registered their identities in the system, *MultiAuth* obtains a trained model capable of authenticating multiple users.

In the authentication stage, multiple users simultaneously perform activities for authentication. The system collects CSI of WiFi signals influenced by the users' activities and employs MUTA to profile the multipath components induced by all users. By aggregating and separating these multipath components, individual CSI profiles for each user are constructed for individual characterization. The trained dual-task model is then utilized to extract behavioral features from user behavior profiles derived from the individual CSI. These features are used to authenticate each user in the multi-user scenario.

4.4 Multi-User Authentication

In this section, we present the design of the multi-user authentication system, *MultiAuth*.

4.4.1 MUTA Implementation for Multipath Profiling

To achieve multi-user authentication, *MultiAuth* first collects CSI of WiFi signals induced by multiple users' activities, and then performs MUTA to profile multipath components of WiFi signals. Due to hardware imperfection and the requirement of subspace construction, *MultiAuth* first needs to calibrate CSI errors and determine multipath numbers before implementing MUTA.

4.4.1.1   CSI Calibration

When collecting CSI data from commodity WiFi devices, it is important to acknowledge the presence of hardware imperfections, which inevitably introduce amplitude and phase errors into the recorded CSI of WiFi signals. These errors arise due to various factors. Amplitude errors occur as a result of digitization errors during the measurement of received signal power. On the other hand, phase errors predominantly stem from clock unsynchronization, including phenomena such as Carrier Frequency Offset (CFO), Sampling Frequency Offset (SFO), and Packet Detection Delay (PDD) [16].

To address and rectify these amplitude and phase errors within the collected CSI data, a calibration process is employed. Specifically, an error correction approach [13] is adopted. The calibration approach first mitigates amplitude errors by averaging raw CSI data obtained from multiple packets collected within the coherence time. This averaging process helps reduce the impact of amplitude errors, resulting in more accurate CSI measurements. Subsequently, constant phase errors are addressed by selecting a reference channel and compensating for the phase differences between each pair of channels. By compensating for these phase differences, the calibration process corrects the phase errors present in the CSI data.

4.4.1.2   Determination of Multipath Number

In MUTA, the number of multipath components is determined by the number of eigenvectors in the signal subspace obtained through eigenvalue decomposition. However, it is crucial to accurately identify the number of multipath components to avoid the inclusion of noise eigenvectors in the signal subspace. Including noise eigenvectors can lead to significant variations in the measured Time of Arrivals (ToAs) across packets, which may impact the detection of user movement.

Since the fluctuations in the Line-of-Sight (LoS) path are solely caused by an inaccurate multipath number, we can utilize the stability of the LoS path to determine the correct number of underlying multipath components within the received CSI. Specifically, in MUTA, pseudo-spectrums are constructed with different multipath numbers, and the variance of the ToAs for the LoS path is calculated over time. The multipath number that results in the minimal variance is selected as the accurate number of multipath components. By setting the accurate multipath number, the fluctuations in the ToAs will only reflect human movement, providing a more reliable representation of user activity.

With the calibrated CSI and an accurate multipath number, *MultiAuth* performs multipath profiling using MUTA mentioned in Sect. 3.2.1.

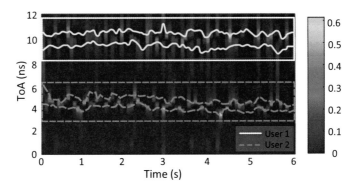

Fig. 4.5 Example of multipath streams

4.4.2 Multipath Aggregation and Separation

Upon implementing MUTA, *MultiAuth* is capable of identifying the multipath components induced by multiple users through the detection of peaks in the pseudo-spectrum. In practical scenarios where the signal has a large bandwidth, it is possible for each individual to reflect multiple multipath components from different body parts. This phenomenon occurs because different body parts can create distinct reflections that manifest as separate multipath components in the signal. To accurately characterize each user, it becomes necessary to aggregate the multipath components associated with each individual and separate the multipath components originating from different individuals.

To facilitate multipath aggregation and separation, *MultiAuth* begins by constructing multipath streams using consecutive pseudo-spectrums after removing static components. Figure 4.5 illustrates an example of multipath streams, showcasing several bright curves representing multipath components over time from the movements of two users. It is evident that multipath components reflected by the same individual are closely aligned, while those between different individuals are further apart. In order to achieve multipath aggregation and separation, *MultiAuth* employs a strategy of aligning curves that are closer together and separating those that are more distant. This process is guided by the energy levels within the spectrogram, as the multipath components associated with users tend to exhibit higher energy. To align the horizontal curves with high energy, dynamic programming techniques are utilized. This alignment procedure helps identify and isolate the multipath components induced by the users. Subsequently, these paths are assigned to different individuals based on the distances between their respective Time of Arrivals (ToAs). The ToA distance of an individual can be set based on the expected range of values for a typical person's movement. By assigning the multipath components to specific ToAs, *MultiAuth* effectively matches the multipath components with their corresponding users.

4.4.3 Individual CSI Construction

After performing multipath aggregation and separation, *MultiAuth* utilizes the resulting multipath components to construct individual Channel State Information (CSI) corresponding to each user within the multi-user scenario. This individual CSI represents the channel conditions specific to each user, capturing information relevant to that particular user from the received CSI. In contrast to the Time of Arrival (ToA) variations that broadly describe user behaviors, the individual CSI simulates the CSI of WiFi signals collected solely from each user. It provides a more precise and accurate characterization of an individual user's channel condition.

To construct each user's individual CSI, we first construct CSI of each multipath component, and then employ all multipath components induced by a user to construct his/her individual CSI. The construction of CSI for each path refers to the estimation of CSI amplitude and phase of the path. Specifically, the CSI $\hat{H}_i$ of the i-th multipath could be expressed as

$$\hat{H}_i = a_i e^{-j(\phi_i + 2\pi f \Delta t_i)}, \tag{4.5}$$

where a_i is the CSI amplitude of i-th path, ϕ_i is the initial phase shift, and $2\pi f \Delta t_i$ is the phase shift caused by the ToA Δt_i under a specific subcarrier f. Theoretically, the sum of CSI for all multipath components should be equal to the actual collected CSI H. Hence, we can estimate CSI of each multipath component by solving an optimization problem, i.e.,

$$[\hat{a}_i, \hat{\phi}_i] = \arg\min_{a_i, \phi_i} \left\| \sum_{i=1}^{N} \hat{H}_i - H \right\|^2, \tag{4.6}$$

where N is the number of multipath components. To solve the above optimization problem, we define the CSI parameters standing for amplitude and initial phase shift as

$$P = [a_1 e^{-j\phi_1} \quad a_2 e^{-j\phi_2} \quad \cdots \quad a_N e^{-j\phi_N}]^T, \tag{4.7}$$

where a_i and ϕ_i denote the amplitude and phase of the i-th multipath. Then, we form phase shifts of multipath's ToAs as

$$\Phi = \begin{bmatrix} e^{-j2\pi f_1 \Delta t_1} & e^{-j2\pi f_1 \Delta t_2} & \cdots & e^{-j2\pi f_1 \Delta t_N} \\ e^{-j2\pi f_2 \Delta t_1} & e^{-j2\pi f_2 \Delta t_2} & \cdots & e^{-j2\pi f_2 \Delta t_N} \\ \cdots & \cdots & \vdots & \cdots \\ e^{-j2\pi f_s \Delta t_1} & e^{-j2\pi f_s \Delta t_2} & \cdots & e^{-j2\pi f_s \Delta t_N} \end{bmatrix} \tag{4.8}$$

where f_i is the frequency of i-th subcarrier and S is the number of subcarriers. Then, the optimization problem can be solved uniquely by the following formula:

$$\hat{P} = (\Phi^T \Phi)^{-1} \Phi^T H. \tag{4.9}$$

Finally, the CSI $\hat{H}_i$ of each multipath component is obtained based on the estimated $\hat{a}_i$ and $\hat{\phi}_i$ in $\hat{P}$, i.e., $\hat{H}_i = \hat{a}_i e^{-j(\hat{\phi}_i + 2\pi f \Delta t_i)}$. After estimating the CSIs for all the multipath components, *MultiAuth* constructs the individual CSI of each user by combining the CSIs of their respective multipath components.

To validate the effectiveness of constructing individual CSI, an experiment is conducted to demonstrate the capability of exhibiting user behaviors using individual CSI. In the experiment, two users are positioned with a vertical distance of 1.5 m and simultaneously perform a pushing hand motion. CSI data are collected from both users and subjected to MUTA to derive individual CSI for each user. Additionally, the CSI of each user is collected in a single-user scenario for comparison. Figure 4.6 depicts the constructed individual CSI in the two-user scenario alongside the CSI collected in the single-user scenario. It is evident that while individual CSIs may exhibit some distortions, their general fluctuation trends align with those observed in the CSIs collected in the single-user scenario. This observation indicates that individual CSI is capable of exhibiting the behaviors of each user solely within multi-user scenarios. The similarity between the individual CSIs and the CSIs collected in the single-user scenario underscores the potential use of individual CSI for achieving multi-user authentication.

4.4.4   *User Behavior Profile Extraction*

Based on the individual Channel State Information (CSI) of each user, *MultiAuth* proceeds to extract user behavior profiles.

Human activities can be represented in CSI streams by two key pieces of information: duration and frequency [11]. Duration refers to the time taken by an individual to perform a particular activity, while frequency represents the velocity of body movements. Due to the inherent physiological and behavioral differences among individuals, users exhibit distinct durations and frequencies in their CSI when engaging in activities. For instance, individuals with high muscle mass tend to exhibit activities with high acceleration and velocity, resulting in shorter durations and higher frequencies. By conducting time-frequency analysis on the CSI data, *MultiAuth* is able to delve deeper into the unique characteristics exhibited by individuals, allowing for effective differentiation and identification of users.

CSI streams of WiFi signals exhibit a similar detection capability to Doppler radar [12], and the Doppler effect can effectively characterize fine-grained movements [3]. To analyze user behaviors, *MultiAuth* utilizes Short-Time Fourier Transform (STFT) to derive time-frequency spectrograms from the individual CSI.

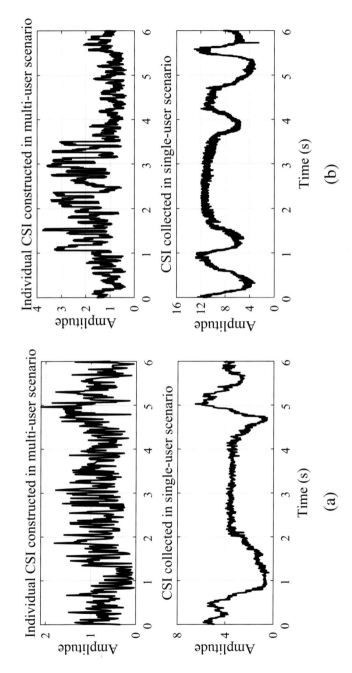

Fig. 4.6 Comparison of individual CSI constructed in multi-user scenario and the CSI collected in single-user scenario. (**a**) User 1. (**b**) User 2

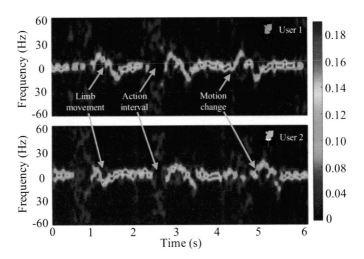

Fig. 4.7 Time-frequency spectrograms for two users

Figure 4.7 illustrates the time-frequency spectrograms generated from the individual CSIs of two users while performing pushing hand motions multiple times. The spectrograms reveal high-energy bands corresponding to the movements of the users' limbs, and the distinct patterns unveils the uniqueness of users' behavior. For example, user 1 displays higher frequency shifts during limb movements, reflecting their faster motion resulting from larger muscle masses. Conversely, user 2 demonstrates longer intervals between actions, reflecting their individual behavioral habits.

To extract user behavior profiles, *MultiAuth* applies a Butterworth filter to eliminate high-frequency noise present in the impulse of individual Channel State Information (CSI). Then, *MultiAuth* performs Short-Time Fourier Transform (STFT) on the filtered individual CSI to obtain time-frequency spectrograms. From these spectrograms, the contours of high-energy bands are calculated. To segment the contours into distinct behavior profiles, *MultiAuth* calculates the magnitude differentials of the contours. The magnitude differential $D(n)$ is computed as follows:

$$D(n) = \sum_{t=nL}^{(n+1)L-1} |C_{t+1} - C_t|, n \in [0, N-1], \tag{4.10}$$

where $D(n)$ is the magnitude differential of the n-th sliding window, L is the length of sliding window, C_t is the contour's magnitude value at time t, and N is the number of sliding window. When $D(n)$ is constantly lower than a predefined threshold, the contour remains stable, which indicates a suspense between actions. Hence, the contour is segmented to episodes in the point, each of which represents a user behavior profile.

4.4.5   Dual-Task Model Construction for User Authentication

The behavior-based authentication process involves two interconnected tasks: identity authentication and activity recognition. There exists shared information between these tasks that can facilitate feature extraction for each task. Instead of designing two independent models to handle these tasks separately, *MultiAuth* employs multi-task learning to construct a dual-task model. This model leverages the shared information between the tasks to learn more fine-grained features for each individual task. Borrow the idea of [2], we design a Convolutional Neural Network-Recurrent Neural Network (CNN-RNN)-based dual-task model to extract robust and fine-grained features for user authentication.

Figure 4.8 illustrates the architecture of the CNN-RNN-based dual-task model. The model comprises a shared feature extractor, which is based on a combination of Convolutional Neural Networks (CNNs) and Recurrent Neural Networks (RNNs), as well as two separate fully-connected networks for the activity recognizer and user authenticator tasks. The feature extractor incorporates three CNNs and two RNNs to extract behavioral features from the input user behavior profile I. The CNNs are composed of convolutional layers abstracting the input I as compressed representation through convolutional operations, and the pooling layers reducing the dimension of the compressed representation. It treats user behavior profiles as images to abstract fine-grained features from pixels to characterize human behaviors. The RNNs partition the feature map from CNNs into fragments for sequential relationship access, and then extracts a feature map R, which embeds the behavioral features underlying human behavior profiles.

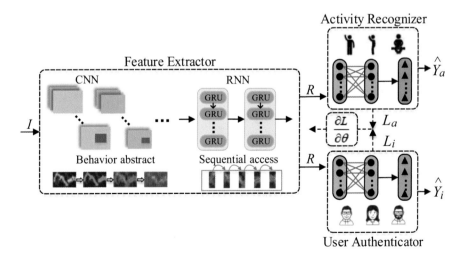

Fig. 4.8 Architecture of CNN-RNN-based dual-task model

The user authenticator and activity recognizer have the same structure, consisting of two FC layers followed by a softmax layer. Both networks take the feature map R extracted from the feature extractor as input. They extract feature representations on different scales to achieve user authentication and activity recognition, respectively. The user authenticator network outputs the identity label $\hat{Y}_i$ and the identity loss L_i, which represents the error of user authentication. On the other hand, the activity recognizer network outputs the activity label $\hat{Y}_a$ and the activity loss L_a, representing the error of activity recognition. To share the information they learn, the two losses are combined for jointly training the model, i.e.,

$$L = \alpha(L_a + b) + \beta e^{(L_i + c)}, \tag{4.11}$$

where α and β are the weights assigned to the activity loss and identity loss, respectively. The parameters b and c are biases for the activity loss and identity loss, respectively. The use of an exponential function in the identity loss allows for a higher emphasis on the convergence of identity loss compared to the activity loss, as user authentication typically requires more nuanced and in-depth features. By continuously backpropagating the gradient of the overall loss $\frac{\partial L}{\partial \theta}$ to the feature extractor, the dual-task model can be trained to extract robust and fine-grained features for both user authentication and activity recognition tasks.

In addition to authenticating legitimate users, *MultiAuth* also incorporates a spoofer detection mechanism to identify unexpected spoofers in multi-user scenarios under the zero-effort attack and imitation attack. As human behavioral features are influenced by both subjective factors (such as personal habits and styles) and objective physiological characteristics (such as limb length and muscle power), there are distinct differences in behavioral features between a spoofer and a legitimate user, even if the spoofer tries to imitate the extrinsic behaviors of the legitimate user. *MultiAuth* leverages these differences to detect spoofers individually in multi-user scenarios. For each user, it compares the identity probabilities $\hat{Y}_i$ across all identity classes with a predefined threshold λ. If all elements in $\hat{Y}_i$ are below the threshold, i.e., $\forall k \in [1, n]$, $Y_i^k < \lambda$, the current user is identified as a spoofer.

4.5   Evaluation

To comprehensively evaluate *MultiAuth*, we conduct experiments in real environments.

4.5.1   Evaluation Setup

To evaluate the performance of *MultiAuth* comprehensively, we conduct real-world experiments in a controlled environment. *MultiAuth* is implemented on an HP

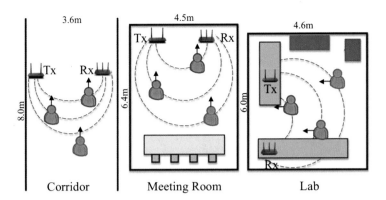

Fig. 4.9 Experimental environments

Pavilion 14 laptop, utilizing two wireless routers equipped with Atheros NIC and three antennas: TL-WDR4310 and TL-WR2543N, respectively. The wireless routers are modified using the Atheros CSI Tool [13], which allows for fast channel switching and the collection of CSI on a larger bandwidth of WiFi signals. Two different signal modes are employed to evaluate the system's performance. In the 2.4 GHz WiFi band, we splice a 70 MHz bandwidth signal from channels 1 to 11, following the methodology outlined in [16]. In the 5 GHz WiFi band, we splice a 200 MHz bandwidth signal from channels 36 to 56, following the methodology presented in [13]. To construct a large measurement matrix, we concatenate the CSI measurement matrices from the three antennas together.

For the experiments, a total of 30 volunteers participate, including 17 males and 13 females. Among them, 20 volunteers act as legitimate users, while the remaining 10 volunteers act as spoofers. Six common activities are selected for the experiments: walking, turning right, turning left, sitting down, standing up, and hands reaching out and pulling back. These activities are performed by the volunteers in three different environments: a corridor, a meeting room, and a lab. The layouts of these environments can be seen in Fig. 4.9. During the experiments, the users perform their activities in specific areas within each environment. The lengths of the propagation path, which includes the human body, the transmitter (Tx), and the receiver (Rx), vary for each user. The orientation of the activities was towards the transceivers. The users do not interfere with the direct signal propagation between other users and the transceivers. This ensures that the signal propagation from other users has minimal influence on the measurements, thereby meeting the basic requirement of the proposed multipath profiling method.

In the register stage, each legitimate volunteer performs each activity 15 times to provide training samples for identity registration. In the authentication stage, the volunteers participate in three different experimental cases: the 1-user case, the 2-user case, and the 3-user case. In the 1-user case, each volunteer is authenticated individually to evaluate the single-user authentication capability of *MultiAuth*. In

Fig. 4.10 Overall performance of *MultiAuth* in different user cases. (**a**) Authentication accuracy in different user cases. (**b**) FAR and FRR in different user cases

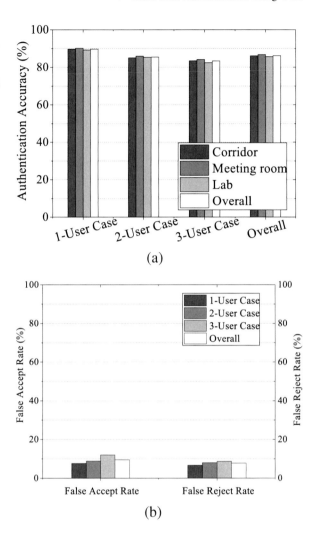

(a)

(b)

the 2-user or 3-user cases, 2 or 3 volunteers are authenticated simultaneously to evaluate the multi-user authentication capability of *MultiAuth*.

4.5.2 Overall Performance

The user authentication performance of *MultiAuth* is evaluated in three different environments, and the results are shown in Fig. 4.10a. In the 1-user case, *MultiAuth* achieved an authentication accuracy of 89.7%. In the 2-user case, the accuracy was 85.5%, and in the 3-user case, the accuracy was 83.4%. On average, *Multi-Auth* achieved an authentication accuracy of 86.2%. The results demonstrate that

Table 4.1 Authentication accuracy under each activity

Activity	Accuracy	Activity	Accuracy
Walking	88.6%	Turning right	87.6%
Turning left	86.9%	Sitting down	85.0%
Stand up	84.6%	Hands out and back	84.5%

MultiAuth is capable of effectively extending single-user authentication to multi-user scenarios while maintaining an acceptable level of authentication performance. Additionally, the small variance in authentication accuracy across different environments indicates the reliability and robustness of *MultiAuth* in various environmental layouts.

The false accept rate (FAR) and false reject rate (FRR) are important metrics to evaluate the performance of *MultiAuth* in detecting spoofers and correctly identifying legitimate users. The results for FAR and FRR under the three cases are shown in Fig. 4.10b. Overall, *MultiAuth* achieves a FAR of 9.5% and an FRR of 7.8%. When compared with the single-user scenario, the FAR and FRR for multi-user scenarios increase by less than 5%, which is considered insignificant. These results demonstrate that *MultiAuth* is reliable in detecting spoofers and resistant to zero-effort and imitation attacks in multi-user scenarios. Additionally, *MultiAuth* maintains a low rate of rejecting legitimate users, ensuring a user-friendly experience.

We further evaluate the authentication accuracy of *MultiAuth* for each activity. The authentication accuracy for each activity is presented in Table 4.1, where the accuracy represents the overall performance across all cases. It can be observed that there are variations in the authentication accuracy among different activities. For example, the walking activity achieves the highest performance, exceeding 88% accuracy. On the other hand, activities such as hands reaching out and pulling back show lower performance. This difference can be attributed to the complexity and diversity of the walking activity, which provides more intrinsic uniqueness through a series of movements.

We further evaluate the authentication accuracy of *MultiAuth* for users with similar physiques. In the experiment, we divide the volunteers into 6 categories, where users within each category have similar physiques. We then evaluate the authentication accuracy for users within each category separately. The authentication accuracy for the 1-user, 2-user, and 3-user cases within each category is 87.4, 83.7, and 82.0%, respectively, with deviations of 2.6, 3.7, and 3.8% within each category. The difference between the authentication accuracy of similarly physical users and that of all users is only 1.9%. This result demonstrates the effectiveness of *MultiAuth* in authenticating users with similar physiques, as it can accurately distinguish users even within groups that have similar physical characteristics.

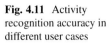
Fig. 4.11 Activity recognition accuracy in different user cases

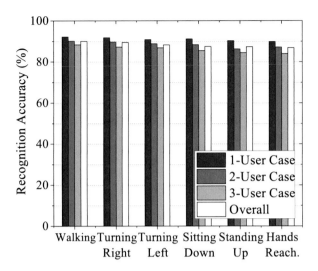

4.5.3   Performance of Activity Recognition

The recognition accuracy for each activity in different cases is shown in Fig. 4.11. The activity recognition accuracies for the three cases are 90.8, 88.1, and 86.0% respectively. These accuracies indicate that recognizing multiple users' activities does not significantly degrade the performance compared to single-user activity recognition. Furthermore, we observe that different activities do not exhibit significant differences in recognition accuracy. This demonstrates that *MultiAuth* can effectively recognize various types of daily activities in multi-user scenarios.

4.5.4   Impact of Horizontal Distance Between Users

We conduct experiments to evaluate the impact of vertical distance between users on multi-user authentication in a 3-user case. The users are categorized as a close user, middle user, and distant user based on their relative distance to the Line of Sight (LOS) path. The close user is positioned at a fixed location, while the middle user and distant user are positioned at varying vertical distances from the close user. For instance, if the vertical distance is set to 0.3 m, it means that the middle user and distant user are respectively located 0.3 and 0.6 m away from the close user vertically. By varying the vertical distance between users, we can assess how it impacts the accuracy of multi-user authentication.

Figure 4.12 shows the authentication accuracy under different distances between users. It can be observed that as the distance between users increases, the overall authentication accuracy improves rapidly and reaches around 80% when the distance reaches 0.6 m. This improvement is due to the increased separation between

Fig. 4.12 Authentication accuracy in different distances

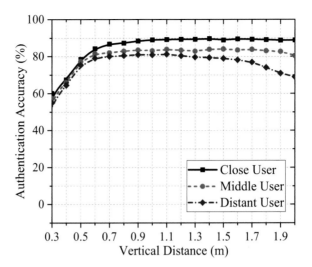

the multipath components of different users, which allows for more accurate identification. However, as the distance exceeds 1.5 m, the authentication accuracy for the distant user starts to decrease gradually due to signal attenuation over long distances. It is worth noting that the suitable face-to-face communication distances between users, as indicated in [8], typically range from 0.46 to 1.22 m. Therefore, *MultiAuth* demonstrates effective multi-user identification capabilities within the majority of suitable communication distances.

4.5.5 Comparison with SOTA Methods

We conduct two experiments to compare the system with two State-Of-The-Art (SOTA) methods.

4.5.5.1 Comparison with *MultiTrack*

First, we compare our system with *MultiTrack* [9] in terms of multi-user activity recognition. *MultiTrack* synthesizes wide bandwidth WiFi signals collected from multiple receivers and utilizes inverse Fast Fourier Transform (IFFT) to derive the power delay profile for multi-user activity recognition. Since our system and *MultiTrack* are implemented on different devices, we conducted two separate groups of experiments, each following the specific experimental requirements of the respective system. We then analyzed the statistical results of the evaluations to compare the performance of the two systems.

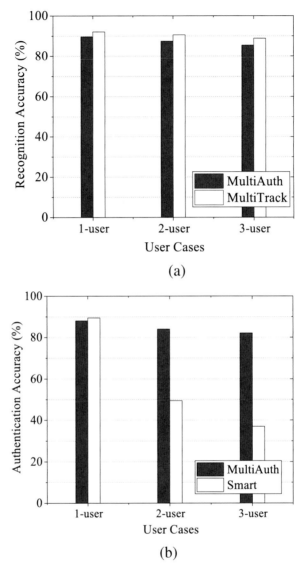

Fig. 4.13 Comparison with SOTA methods. (**a**) Activity recognition accuracy of *MultiAuth* and *MultiTrack*. (**b**) User authentication accuracy of *MultiAuth* and *Smart*

The accuracy of multi-user activity recognition for our system and *MultiTrack* is presented in Fig. 4.13a. Both systems demonstrate the ability to effectively recognize the predefined activities. Specifically, in three-user cases, our proposed system, *MultiAuth*, achieves accuracy rates of 89.7, 87.5, and 85.5%, while *MultiTrack* achieves rates of 92.1, 90.6, and 88.9% respectively. Compared to *MultiTrack*, our system exhibits a slight decrease in accuracy of 2.4, 3.1, and 3.4% respectively.

Despite utilizing only a single pair of transceivers, our system achieves comparable performance to *MultiTrack* in activity recognition. These results demonstrate the effectiveness of our proposed algorithms in separating multipath components and extracting individual features using a single pair of transceivers.

4.5.5.2 Comparison with *Smart*

We compare authentication accuracy of the proposed system with a single-user authentication approach, *Smart* [7]. This work exploits statistical features of CSI in time and frequency domains collected from a single receiver for user authentication. In the evaluation, we collect WiFi signals following the setup requirement of *Smart* and our system respectively. The multi-user scenarios of *Smart* are the same as *MultiAuth*, i.e., two or three users are located in specific positions and perform the activities. The authentication accuracy of *Smart* under multi-user scenarios is calculated by the probability that any of the users is successfully identified. Based on the two groups of evaluation, we analyze statistical results for comparing the two systems.

Figure 4.13b shows the authentication accuracy for *MultiAuth* and *Smart* respectively. We can observe that the performance of *Smart* in multi-user scenarios drops significantly by 34.6 and 45.1%. This demonstrates the effectiveness of *MultiAuth* in handling authentication in multi-user scenarios. From the perspective of single-user authentication, *MultiAuth* achieves similar performance to *Smart*. This indicates that the proposed *MultiAuth* system can effectively authenticate users in both single-user and multi-user scenarios.

4.5.6 Impact of User Location

In the experiment, we evaluate the impact of user location on the performance of the *MultiAuth* system. Three representative scenarios of user locations on one side are considered: Scenario A, Scenario B, and Scenario C, as shown in Fig. 4.14a. Scenario A and Scenario B are typical setups used in previous evaluations, where the signal propagation between users is non-obstructed and interference-free. These scenarios allow for reliable signal transmission and propagation. Scenario C represents a more challenging setup, where the users are located in a straight line with connected propagation paths. In this scenario, the signal propagation between users is affected by interference and obstruction. The vertical distances between users range from 0.8 to 1.2 m.

Performance under the three scenarios for 3-user cases is shown in Fig. 4.14b. For scenarios A and B, where the signal propagation between users is non-obstructed and interference-free, *MultiAuth* achieves acceptable accuracy of 85.9 and 85.2% respectively. Moreover, the variation in authentication accuracy among different users in these scenarios is insignificant, demonstrating a robust authentication

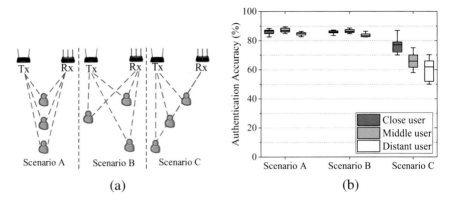

Fig. 4.14 Setup and performance for different locations. (**a**) Setup of user location. (**b**) Authentication accuracy under different locations

performance. On the other hand, in scenario C, the authentication accuracy for the three users dramatically decreases. The front user acts as an obstacle, interfering with the signal propagation of the back users. As a result, the authentication accuracy decreases to 77.4, 65.3, and 62.2% for the three users respectively with significant variations among users. These results indicate that the authentication capability is affected in scenarios where users obstruct the signal propagation of other users.

4.5.7 Impact of Signal Bandwidth

Signal bandwidth determines the number of available subcarriers in MUTA and affects the resolution of multipath profiling. To evaluate the impact of signal bandwidth, we implement *MultiAuth* with varying signal bandwidths ranging from 20 to 60 MHz under the 2.4 GHz signal and 80 to 200 MHz under the 5 GHz signal. Figure 4.15 shows the authentication accuracy of different cases under these bandwidths. It can be observed that larger bandwidths lead to improved authentication accuracy for all cases. Specifically, as the bandwidth increases from 20 to 200 MHz, the overall authentication accuracy for the three cases improves from 53.1 to 86.2%. The reason for this improvement is that a larger bandwidth allows for the resolution of more multipath components. With a sufficient number of subcarriers, MUTA can effectively characterize each individual user's multipath components, resulting in a more accurate and reliable authentication process.

Fig. 4.15 Authentication accuracy under different bandwidths

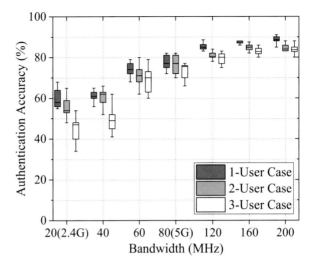

Fig. 4.16 Authentication accuracy under different antenna numbers

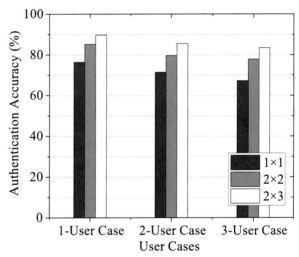

4.5.8 Impact of Antenna Number

To evaluate the impact of antenna numbers, different numbers of antennas are utilized in the transmitter and receiver to establish different transmissions: 1×1, 2×2, and 2×3 transmissions. These transmissions result in measurement matrices of different sizes in the *MultiAuth* system for multipath profiling. Figure 4.16 shows the authentication accuracy of *MultiAuth* under different transmissions. It can be observed that when using a 1×1 transmission, the authentication accuracy is 71.6% on average. However, as the number of antennas increases, i.e., more transmission links are utilized, the authentication accuracy also increases. With the use of 2×2 and 2×3 transmissions, the authentication accuracy reaches 80.8 and 86.2%

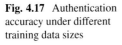

Fig. 4.17 Authentication accuracy under different training data sizes

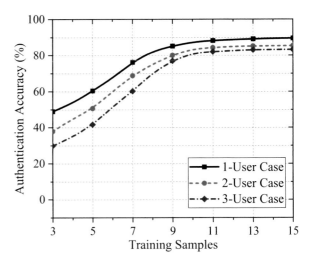

respectively. These results demonstrate that by constructing a larger measurement matrix using more antennas, *MultiAuth* improves the spatial resolution and better characterizes each user in multi-user scenarios.

4.5.9   Impact of Training Data Size

We analyze the authentication accuracy of *MultiAuth* under different training data sizes for the three cases. Figure 4.17 shows the authentication accuracy of *MultiAuth* as the training data size increases. It can be observed that as the training data size increases, the authentication accuracy initially improves and then tends to stabilize for all the cases. When the training data size reaches 9 samples, the authentication accuracies for the three cases increase to 85.1, 80.5, and 78.3% respectively. Hence, a training data size of at least 9 samples per user per activity is required to achieve an acceptable multi-user authentication performance, which does not significantly affect user experience during user registration.

4.6   Conclusion

In this chapter, we study the problem of multi-user authentication using WiFi signal sensing. We propose a multi-user authentication system, *MultiAuth*, which can utilize a single pair of WiFi devices to sense multiple users for user authentication. We first propose a multipath time of arrival measurement algorithm to profile multipath components of WiFi signals in multi-user sensing scenarios. Then, we construct individual CSI to characterize each user individually, and design a neural network model to extract behavioral features for user authentication. Extensive experiments in real multi-user scenarios demonstrate the effectiveness of multi-user authentication.

References

1. Duarte, M., Sabharwal, A., Aggarwal, V., Jana, R., Ramakrishnan, K.K., Rice, C.W., Shankara-narayanan, N.K.: Design and characterization of a full-duplex multiantenna system for wifi networks. IEEE Trans. Veh. Technol. **63**(3), 1160–1177 (2014)
2. Li, C., Liu, M., Cao, Z.: Wihf: enable user identified gesture recognition with wifi. In: Proceedings of IEEE INFOCOM'20, Toronto, pp. 586–595 (2020)
3. Lu, L., Yu, J., Chen, Y., Zhu, Y., Xu, X., Xue, G., Li, M.: Keylistener: inferring keystrokes on QWERTY keyboard of touch screen through acoustic signals. In: Proceedings of IEEE INFOCOM'19, France, pp. 775–783 (2019)
4. Miraz, M.H., Ali, M., Excell, P.S., Picking, R.: A review on internet of things (IoT), internet of everything (IoE) and internet of nano things (IonT). In: 2015 Internet Technologies and Applications (ITA), pp. 219–224. IEEE, Piscataway (2015)
5. Schmidt, R.: Multiple emitter location and signal parameter estimation. IEEE Trans. Antennas Propag. **34**(3), 276–280 (1986)
6. Shahzad, M., Zhang, S.: Augmenting user identification with wifi based gesture recognition. Proc. ACM Interact. Mob. Wearable Ubiquitous Technol. **2**(3), 134 (2018)
7. Shi, C., Liu, J., Liu, H., Chen, Y.: Smart user authentication through actuation of daily activities leveraging wifi-enabled IoT. In: Proceedings of ACM MobiHoc'17, Chennai, p. 5 (2017)
8. Sorokowska, A., Sorokowski, P., Hilpert, P., Cantarero, K., Frackowiak, T., Ahmadi, K., Alghraibeh, A.M., Aryeetey, R., Bertoni, A., Bettache, K., et al.: Preferred interpersonal distances: a global comparison. J. Cross-Cultural Psychol. **48**(4), 577–592 (2017)
9. Tan, S., Zhang, L., Wang, Z., Yang, J.: Multitrack: multi-user tracking and activity recognition using commodity wifi. In: Proceedings of ACM CHI'19, Glasgow, p. 536 (2019)
10. Tulino, A.M., Lozano, A., Verdú, S.: Impact of antenna correlation on the capacity of multiantenna channels. IEEE Trans. Inf. Theory **51**(7), 2491–2509 (2005)
11. Wang, W., Liu, A.X., Shahzad, M., Ling, K., Lu, S.: Understanding and modeling of wifi signal based human activity recognition. In: Proceedings of ACM MobiCom'15, New York (2015)
12. Wang, W., Liu, A.X., Shahzad, M.: Gait recognition using wifi signals. In: Proceedings of ACM UbiComp'16, Heidelberg, pp. 363–373 (2016)
13. Xie, Y., Li, Z., Li, M.: Precise power delay profiling with commodity wifi. In: Proceedings of ACM MobiCom'15, Paris, pp. 53–64 (2015)
14. Zeng, Y., Pathak, P.H., Mohapatra, P.: Wiwho: wifi-based person identification in smart spaces. In: Proceedings of IEEE IPSN'16, Vienna, p. 4 (2016)
15. Zhou, C., Haber, F., Jaggard, D.L.: A resolution measure for the MUSIC algorithm and its application to plane wave arrivals contaminated by coherent interference. IEEE Trans. Signal Process. **39**(2), 454–463 (1991)
16. Zhuo, Y., Zhu, H., Xue, H., Chang, S.: Perceiving accurate CSI phases with commodity wifi devices. In: Proceedings of IEEE INFOCOM'17, pp. 1–9 (2017)

Chapter 5
State-of-Art Research

Abstract In this chapter, we review state-of-the-art research related to WiFi signal-based user authentication. We first survey mainstream user authentication approaches. Then, we investigate WiFi signal sensing research, and further review the latest WiFi signal-based user authentication work. Finally, we give a summary of existing research.

Keywords User authentication · WiFi signal sensing · WiFi signal-based user authentication

5.1 User Authentication Research

Traditional user authentication methods still play an important role in traditional scenarios and IoT environments. Password [14] is the most traditional and widely used identification method. In order to overcome the lengthy nature of passwords, the shorter personal identification number (PIN) has gradually replaced the status of passwords in some scenarios, and gradually become the "unlock" tool for many electronic devices. However, whether it is based on password or PIN, it is a "knowledge" based user authentication method, which is easy to be forgotten and affect the use of users. In addition, these traditional identification methods are easy to be leaked, making them difficult to resist theft attacks, and security is greatly compromised.

Biometrics-based user authentication exploits human biometric characteristics to authenticate user identity, including fingerprint, face, iris and vocal print, etc. It has become one of the most widely used authentication methods at present, which has contributed to the emergence of a large number of commercial products. Fingerprint recognition [5, 15] scans the unique fingerprint pattern of each individual through the comparison with the pre-stored fingerprint template to identify, which is widely used in mobile phone unlock and access control system. Despite their ease of use and accessibility, fingerprints can be contaminated or damaged, making them unidentifiable and at risk of being copied. Face recognition [3, 8, 13, 20] is another widely used authentication method that authenticates users by identifying key

J. Yu et al., *WiFi signal-based user authentication*, SpringerBriefs in Computer Science, https://doi.org/10.1007/978-981-99-5914-3_5

biometric features in the human face. Face recognition is simple to operate, easy to use, high accuracy, but it is easy to be affected by factors such as lighting, angle, occlusion and noise. Iris recognition [33] collects images of the iris of the human eye as a unique physiological feature for authentication. Iris recognition accuracy is high because the iris is one of the most stable and unique biometric features in the human body. However, it requires the user to cooperate to achieve close eye scanning, affecting the user experience, and the recognition equipment is more expensive. In addition, vocal print recognition [6, 37] has gradually attracted widespread attention. However, it is prone to interference in noisy environments, and is also vulnerable to simple replay attacks and complex speech synthesis attacks.

5.2   WiFi Signal Sensing Research

Due to the widespread presence of signals in indoor environments, WiFi signal-based positioning has the natural advantage of being deployed in indoor environments. Some of the early work utilizes WiFi fingerprints for device-oriented positioning. The principle of the fingerprint-based method is that the features extracted from the WiFi signal are contextual, and the WiFi waveform or value is related to the location and orientation of the device. Fingerprinting methods can use CSI [21, 30] or RSS [4] to achieve positioning. In addition to the method based on WiFi fingerprints, angle of arrival (AoA)-based indoor positioning [7, 34] has been favored by researchers. In addition to device-oriented indoor positioning, device-free indoor positioning methods have also gained a lot of research and contributed to the emergence of many practical applications. For example, MaTrack [10] is an AoA based device-independent passive user targeting method that utilizes the shift of peaks in the AoA spectrum to locate the target. Widar [17] proposes a geometric modeling method to quantify the relationship between changes in CSI and the user's location and speed, achieving simultaneous estimation of human movement speed, direction, and location at the decimeter level. Widar2.0 [19] builds a unified model to calculate AoA, time of flight (ToF) and Doppler shift (DFS) for passive user location and tracking.

The recognition of human behavior is the key factor to realize efficient and intelligent human-computer interaction. CARM [25] uses principal component analysis (PCA) and discrete wavelet transform (DWT) for feature extraction, and adopts the method based on Hidden Markov model (HMM) to realize daily behavior recognition. E-eyes [24] realizes the construction of semi-supervised behavioral action signal pattern, and can be updated adaptively to adapt to the movement of equipment and daily signal calibration, which realizes the recognition of common behavioral actions. WiHear [26] senses the motion profile of the human mouth through WiFi and uses partial multipath effect and wavelet packet transformation to realize micro-motion detection, which can "hear" people's conversation within the WiFi sensing range. WiFinger [9] realizes gesture recognition by sensing subtle finger movements through unique patterns in WiFi signal CSI. WiKey [2] uses WiFi signals to sense keyboard strokes and identify the unique pattern of fingers for each key to achieve key recognition and input content tracking. WiDance [18] proposes a motion direction prediction technique that can detect, segment and recognize motion without training. Widar3.0 [39] builds a speed profile for the cross-domain problem of WiFi perception, and realizes behavior recognition without training in new scenarios.

In recent years, the health monitoring of family members has become a hot spot of social concern, including the action monitoring of children and the elderly, and the vital signs monitoring. When a child or an elderly person falls, it can have an instantaneous and significant impact on the spread of the WiFi signal. By analyzing the changes in the WiFi signal, it can judge whether the user has fallen, so as to immediately issue an alarm or notification. Some work [16, 28, 31] has implemented fall detection based on WiFi signals using the signal changes of CSI (e.g. amplitude and phase). The WiFi signal can sense the breathing movement of the human body, so as to monitor the user's breathing state and sleep state. UbiBreathe [1] detects periodic breathing of variance based on signal strength and designs a sleep apnea detection system based on estimated respiratory rate. Liu et al. [12] demonstrated that CSI amplitudes can be used to monitor heart rate and respiratory cycle. Wang et al. [27] introduced the Fresnel zone perception model to convert chest displacement into phase change for more accurate respiration measurements.

5.3 WiFi Signal-Based User Authentication

Due to the widespread demand for wireless local area networks and the popularization and development of WiFi technology, WiFi signals have become ubiquitous in indoor environments. The perception based on WiFi signal does not have the same strong privacy leakage problem as the visual method, and it is not limited by lighting conditions. The strength have prompted the emergence of WiFi signal-based user authentication. WiFi signal-based user authentication refers to the technology that leverage WiFi signals to capture human behavioral features for authenticating users.

Walking is one of the most common daily activities. Based on the walking process of stride length, frequency, gait and other habits, we can reveal the uniqueness of the user's behavior. Some work uses WiFi signal to sense the user's walking gait for user authentication. For example, WifiU [29] extracts gait patterns in the spectral graph from CSI of WiFi signals. WiWho [35] combines the time and frequency characteristics of CSI to authenticate user identity. Wifi-id [36] constructed an identity recognition system based on sensing disturbances in the WiFi spectrum of human gait. WiDIGR [38] uses Fresnel model to construct direction-independent signal spectrum under WiFi signal perception to realize user identification under different walking trajectories. Wipin [32] leverages WiFi signal perception under stationary state of users, including body shape, body fat rate, body features to authenticate user identity. However, neither the walking action nor the static state can express the specific interaction semantics in the Internet of Things, and it is difficult to support the needs of identity identification and authentication in IoT scenario.

In addition to human gait, human daily activities can also be used for authentication. Shi et al. [23] use WiFi signals to sense daily activities, such as eating, cleaning, opening doors and walking, and build a deep neural network to extract behavioral characteristics to achieve user authentication in a more natural state. WiID [22] designs a plug-and-play user behavior-based authentication method to extract timing features of motion speed from WiFi signal CSI, and further extracts individual specificity from it to distinguish different users. WIHF [11] constructs a cross-domain motion pattern under arm movement, and combines deep neural network to realize user identification.

5.4 Summary of Existing Research

In this chapter, we investigate related research work focusing on user authentication, WiFi signal sensing, and WiFi signal-based user authentication. In user authentication research, most of the existing work relies on traditional authentication methods or biometric authentication methods, resulting in security threats such as theft attacks and replay attacks. Differently, the WiFi signal-based authentication research are novel and can resit various theft and replay attacks. However, most of these WiFi signal-based authentication work requires users to perform specific behavioral actions, which makes the existing work has certain limitations at the behavioral level. At the same time, most of the existing work has not considered the identity recognition problem in the case of environment, location and direction change, which makes it have corresponding constraints at the scene level. Therefore, prior to this book, no work has considered WiFi signal-based authentication in diverse behaviors and complex scenes. Compared with the existing research work, this book explores the WiFi signal-based identity recognition technology in the variable and complex scenes for the first time, reducing the limitations of behavior and expanding the usability of behavior, improving the practicability in the variable background and expanding the multi-person scene. The research of this book provides a new solution for the ubiquitous privacy security protection by providing WiFi signal-based user authentication capability for more complex and widely used cases.

References

1. Abdelnasser, H., Harras, K.A., Youssef, M.: Ubibreathe: a ubiquitous non-invasive wifi-based breathing estimator. In: Proceedings of ACM MobiHoc, pp. 277–286. ACM, New York (2015)
2. Ali, K., Liu, A.X., Wang, W., Shahzad, M.: Keystroke recognition using wifi signals. In: Proceedings of ACM MobiCom, pp. 90–102. ACM, New York (2015)

3. Apple: Face id: your face is your password (2017). https://www.apple.com/iphone-xs/face-id/
4. Bahl, P., Padmanabhan, V.N.: Radar: an in-building RF-based user location and tracking system. In: Proceedings of IEEE INFOCOM, vol. 2, pp. 775–784. IEEE, Piscataway (2000)
5. Gragnaniello, D., Poggi, G., Sansone, C., Verdoliva, L.: Local contrast phase descriptor for fingerprint liveness detection. Pattern Recognit. **48**(4), 1050–1058 (2015)
6. Kersta, L.G.: Voiceprint identification. Nature **196**(4861), 1253–1257 (1962)
7. Kotaru, M., Joshi, K., Bharadia, D., Katti, S.: Spotfi: decimeter level localization using wifi. In: Proceedings of ACM SIGCOMM'15, London, pp. 269–282 (2015)
8. Lawrence, S., Giles, C.L., Tsoi, A.C., Back, A.D.: Face recognition: a convolutional neural-network approach. IEEE Trans. Neural Netw. **8**(1), 98–113 (1997)
9. Li, H., Yang, W., Wang, J., Xu, Y., Huang, L.: Wifinger: talk to your smart devices with finger-grained gesture. In: Proceedings of ACM Ubicomp'16, Heidelberg (2016)
10. Li, X., Li, S., Zhang, D., Xiong, J., Wang, Y., Mei, H.: Dynamic-music: accurate device-free indoor localization. In: Proceedings of ACM UbiComp'16, Heidelberg, pp. 196–207 (2016)
11. Li, C., Liu, M., Cao, Z.: Wihf: enable user identified gesture recognition with wifi. In: Proceedings of IEEE INFOCOM'20, Toronto, pp. 586–595 (2020)
12. Liu, J., Wang, Y., Chen, Y., Yang, J., Chen, X., Cheng, J.: Tracking vital signs during sleep leveraging off-the-shelf wifi. In: Proceedings of ACM MobiHoc'15, Hangzhou, pp. 267–276 (2015)
13. Moon, H., Kwon, T.: Biometric person authentication for access control scenario based on face recognition. In: *Proceedings of UAHCI'07*, Beijing (2007)
14. Morris, R., Thompson, K.: Password security: a case history. Commun. ACM **22**(11), 594–597 (1979)
15. Nogueira, R.F., de Alencar Lotufo, R., Machado, R.C.: Fingerprint liveness detection using convolutional neural networks. IEEE Trans. Inf. Forens. Secur. **11**(6), 1206–1213 (2016)
16. Palipana, S., Rojas, D., Agrawal, P., Pesch, D.: Falldefi: ubiquitous fall detection using commodity wi-fi devices. Proc. ACM IMWUT **1**(4), 1–25 (2018)
17. Qian, K., Wu, C., Yang, Z., Liu, Y., Jamieson, K.: Widar: decimeter-level passive tracking via velocity monitoring with commodity wi-fi. In: Proceedings of ACM MobiHoc, pp. 1–10. ACM, New York (2017)
18. Qian, K., Wu, C., Zhou, Z., Zheng, Y., Yang, Z., Liu, Y.: Inferring motion direction using commodity wi-fi for interactive exergames. In: Proceedings of ACM CHI, pp. 1961–1972. ACM, New York (2017)
19. Qian, K., Wu, C., Zhang, Y., Zhang, G., Yang, Z., Liu, Y.: Widar2. 0: passive human tracking with a single wi-fi link. In: Proceedings of ACM MobiSys'18, Munich, pp. 350–361 (2018)
20. Schroff, F., Kalenichenko, D., Philbin, J.: Facenet: a unified embedding for face recognition and clustering. In: Proceedings of IEEE CVPR'15, Boston, pp. 815–823, (2015)
21. Sen, S., Radunovic, B., Choudhury, R.R., Minka, T.: You are facing the mona lisa: spot localization using phy layer information. In: Proceedings of ACM MobiSys, pp. 183–196. ACM, New York (2012)
22. Shahzad, M., Zhang, S.: Augmenting user identification with wifi based gesture recognition. Proc. ACM Interact. Mob. Wearable Ubiquitous Technol. **2**(3), 134 (2018)
23. Shi, C., Liu, J., Liu, H., Chen, Y.: Smart user authentication through actuation of daily activities leveraging wifi-enabled IoT. In: Proceedings of ACM MobiHoc'17, Chennai, p. 5 (2017)
24. Wang, Y., Liu, J., Chen, Y., Gruteser, M., Yang, J., Liu, H.: E-eyes: device-free location-oriented activity identification using fine-grained wifi signatures. In: Proceedings of ACM MobiCom'14, Maui (2014)
25. Wang, W., Liu, A.X., Shahzad, M., Ling, K., Lu, S.: Understanding and modeling of wifi signal based human activity recognition. In: Proceedings of ACM MobiCom'15, New York (2015)
26. Wang, G., Zou, Y., Zhou, Z., Wu, K., Ni, L.M.: We can hear you with wi-fi! IEEE Trans. Mobile Comput. **15**(11), 2907–2920 (2016)
27. Wang, H., Zhang, D., Ma, J., Wang, Y., Wang, Y., Wu, D., Gu, T., Xie, B.: Human respiration detection with commodity wifi devices: do user location and body orientation matter? In: Proceedings of ACM UbiComp, pp. 25–36. ACM, New York (2016)

28. Wang, H., Zhang, D., Wang, Y., Ma, J., Wang, Y., Li, S.: RT-fall: a real-time and contactless fall detection system with commodity wifi devices. IEEE Trans. Mobile Comput. **16**(2), 511–526 (2016)
29. Wang, W., Liu, A.X., Shahzad, M.: Gait recognition using wifi signals. In: Proceedings of ACM UbiComp'16, Heidelberg, pp. 363–373 (2016)
30. Wang, X., Gao, L., Mao, S., Pandey, S.: CSI-based fingerprinting for indoor localization: a deep learning approach. IEEE Trans. Veh. Technol. **66**(1), 763–776 (2016)
31. Wang, Y., Wu, K., Ni, L.M.: Wifall: device-free fall detection by wireless networks. IEEE Trans. Mobile Comput. **16**(2), 581–594 (2016)
32. Wang, F., Han, J., Lin, F., Ren, K.: Wipin: operation-free passive person identification using wi-fi signals. In: Proceedings of IEEE GLOBECOM, pp. 1–6. IEEE, Piscataway (2019)
33. Wildes, R.P.: IRIS recognition: an emerging biometric technology. Proc. IEEE **85**(9), 1348–1363 (1997)
34. Xiong, J., Jamieson, K.: Arraytrack: a fine-grained indoor location system. In: Proceedings of USENIX NSDI, pp. 71–84. USENIX (2013)
35. Zeng, Y., Pathak, P.H., Mohapatra, P.: Wiwho: wifi-based person identification in smart spaces. In: Proceedings of IEEE IPSN'16, Vienna, p. 4 (2016)
36. Zhang, J., Wei, B., Hu, W., Kanhere, S.S.: Wifi-id: human identification using wifi signal. In: Proceedings of IEEE DCOSS'16, Hangzhou, pp. 75–82 (2016)
37. Zhang, L., Tan, S., Yang, J., Chen, Y.: Voicelive: a phoneme localization based liveness detection for voice authentication on smartphones. In: Proceedings of ACM CCS'16, Vienna, pp. 1080–1091 (2016)
38. Zhang, L., Wang, C., Ma, M., Zhang, D.: Widigr: direction-independent gait recognition system using commercial wi-fi devices. IEEE Internet Things J. **7**(2), 1178–1191 (2019)
39. Zheng, Y., Zhang, Y., Qian, K., Zhang, G., Liu, Y., Wu, C., Yang, Z.: Zero-effort cross-domain gesture recognition with wi-fi. In: Proceedings of ACM MobiSys'19, Seoul, pp. 313–325 (2019)

Chapter 6
Summary

Abstract In this chapter, we give a conclusion of this book and summary the contribution. Finally, we give our perspective of future research direction in techniques and application scenarios.

Keywords Internet of things · Low training cost · Sensing expansion · Integrated sensing and communication

6.1 Conclusion of the Book

With the upgrading of mobile devices and the continuous progress of technology, IoT has emerged with the wave of artificial intelligence and has received widespread attention. In IoT environment, user authentication is the key to support various application scenarios, which can provide the privacy security and facilitate various kinds of user-centered intelligent services. The existing authentication methods are either realized through traditional passwords or physical cards, or through biometric features such as faces, fingerprints and vocal prints, which are difficult to support the application scenarios in IoT scenarios. There have been studies that use WiFi signals to sense human behavior characteristics to realize user authentication, but few have considered the variability of behavior and the complexity of scenes. In this book, we study the key technology of WiFi signal-based user authentication, which aims to promote the in-depth integration of user authentication and WiFi signal sensing technology for extensive IoT scenarios.

In Chap. 2, we focus on finger gesture-based user authentication leveraging WiFi signals. A *FingerPass* system is proposed to integrate human computer interaction and user authentication. First, we pre-process and segment CSI of WiFi signals through amplitude differential, and then recognize finger gestures by Support Vector Machine. For highly accurate and real-time user authentication, *FingerPass* divides the whole authentication into two stages, i.e., login and interaction stages. For the login stage, we propose a deep learning-based approach, i.e., Long Short-Term Memory Deep Neural Network, for highly accurate user identification. For the interaction stage, to provide continuous user authentication in real time, a verification mechanism with lightweight classifiers is proposed to continuously authenticate the user during each interaction of finger gestures. Experiments show that *FingerPass* is reliable for continuous user authentication in smart homes.

In Chap. 3, we propose a user authentication system, *FreeAuth*, which leverages WiFi signals to identify individuals in a gesture-independent manner. First, we explore the physiological characteristics underlying body gestures, and find that different individuals exhibit individual differences in the statistical distributions under WiFi signals induced by various body gestures. We propose an adversarial learning-based model, which can suppress the behavioral interferences of body gestures, and extract invariant individual uniqueness unrelated to specific body gestures. With the model, *FreeAuth* can continuously identify individuals through arbitrary body gestures. Experiment results in real indoor environments demonstrate that *FreeAuth* is effective in gesture-independent user authentication.

In Chap. 4, we propose *MultiAuth* which could authenticate multiple users with commodity WiFi device. We first present a MUltipath Time of Arrival measurement algorithm (MUTA) to profile multipath components of WiFi signals in high resolution. Then, after aggregating and separating the multipath components reflected by different users, we construct individual CSI of each user for behavior characterization. Afterward, we extract user behavior profiles from individual CSI, and further design a Convolutional Neural Network-Recurrent Neural Network (CNN-RNN)-based dual-task model to authenticate each user under multi-user scenarios. Experiments demonstrate that *MultiAuth* is accurate and reliable for multi-user authentication.

6.2 Future Direction

With the continuous extension of the application scenarios of IoT, privacy security has become a key consideration and caused an urgent need for user authentication. Under this trend, combined with the research content of the book, more in-depth and extensive research may be conducted in the following directions in the future. The future research prospects of this paper are as follows:

Model Construction with Low Training Cost Nowadays, a large number of WiFi signal-based sensing applications are implemented based on the powerful capabilities of neural networks. Therefore, these applications have a training process in which labeled data is fed into the model to learn how to extract feature representations and give predictions. In general, better performance can be achieved by increasing the amount of training data. However, with the increasing complexity, diversification, and specialization of sensing applications, it is increasingly difficult to obtain appropriate and sufficient training data. In addition, although there are some common data sets [5], the large dedicated data sets for various RF signals in the iot environment are not enough to support increasingly complex applications. In order to reduce the heavy training burden of RF signal sensing applications, this paper proposes a small sample learning method based on knowledge distillation [1]. Other work proposes an approach for cross-modal conversion [4] that utilizes existing large visual datasets to generate WiFi signals for training, reducing the need for large WiFi signal datasets. Other efforts rely on more efficient data representation [2] for small sample learning. However, the applicability of these approaches to various smart IoT applications with different intermediate representation and learning tasks varies. For future research, methods such as transfer learning [3] can be considered to replace the traditional model building process in order to reduce the workload of model training in sensing tasks.

The Expansion of Sensing Space, Sensing Equipment and Sensing Ability The smart Internet of Things is usually built in various indoor environments, constituting a variety of intelligent indoor environments such as smart homes, smart offices, smart factories, and smart shopping malls. As more and more outdoor environments also continue to integrate wireless communication or mobile communication systems, WiFi signals are becoming more and more common outdoors. Therefore, we can further study the perception application in the outdoor environment, which can meet the use needs in a wider range of scenarios, and provide users with whole-process, continuous and universal intelligent services. In addition, with the further development of IoT technology and expansion of mobile devices, more and more devices integrate RF components, and especially strengthen the data storage capacity and computing power. Therefore, the sensing technology based on WiFi signals can be extended to these new IoT devices, or the sensing ability of multiple devices can be combined to complete more complex SENSING tasks, so as to make full use of wireless sensing facilities to form a more intelligent and powerful IoT environment.

The Realization of Integrated Sensing and Communication The rapid growth of 5G and 6G networks is enabling higher frequency bands and larger antenna arrays for wireless communications, while also enabling more precise and high-resolution sensing based on emerging wireless communication technologies. Therefore, future research should not only focus on communication or perception, but should integrate sensing and communication, leading to the realization of Integrated Sensing and Communication (ISAC), which can combine the advantages of sensing and communication to provide ubiquitous sensing services while enabling more efficient communication. There has been some work focused on the implementation of ISAC. For example, some work has addressed the integration of sensing and communication in cellular MIMO systems to provide high-quality services. However, in smart home, smart office, smart manufacturing and other environments, ISAC is still a problem to be further studied. For example, in indoor environments, the number of wireless signal devices per type is usually small, making existing ISAC solutions for massive MIMO unsuitable for indoor environments. Therefore, it is possible to further study how to implement ISAC in a single type of wireless device with a limited number of devices, or to effectively implement ISAC with different types of wireless devices.

References

1. Hinton, G., Vinyals, O., Dean, J.: Distilling the knowledge in a neural network (2015). arXiv:1503.02531
2. Ozturk, M.Z., Wu, C., Wang, B., Liu, K.J.R.: Gaitcube: deep data cube learning for human recognition with millimeter-wave radio. IEEE Internet Things J. **9**(1), 546–557 (2021)
3. Pan, S.J., Yang, Q.: A survey on transfer learning. IEEE Trans. Knowl. Data Eng. **22**(10), 1345–1359 (2010)
4. Xu, W., Song, W., Liu, J., Liu, Y., Cui, X., Zheng, Y., Han, J., Wang, X., Ren, K.: Mask does not matter: anti-spoofing face authentication using mmwave without on-site registration. In: Proceedings of ACM MobiCom, pp. 310–323. ACM, New York (2022)
5. Zheng, Y., Zhang, Y., Qian, K., Zhang, G., Liu, Y., Wu, C., Yang, Z.: Zero-effort cross-domain gesture recognition with wi-fi. In: Proceedings of ACM MobiSys'19, Seoul, pp. 313–325 (2019)

Printed in the United States
by Baker & Taylor Publisher Services